The Inner Splendor

THE INNER SPLENDOR

BOOKS BY DR. DUNNINGTON

The Inner Splendor
Handles of Power
More Handles of Power
Start Where You Are
Something to Stand On
Keys to Richer Living

THE INNER SPLENDOR

by

LEWIS L. DUNNINGTON

New York — 1954

THE MACMILLAN COMPANY

Printed in the United States of America

First Printing

This book is lovingly dedicated to our grandchildren—little experts at calling forth the Inner Splendor in all who know them.

My deep gratitude is hereby tendered to Evelyn Faucett for her painstaking care in the preparation of this manuscript.

L. L. D.

A Personal Word

Eleven years ago, I authored a book called *Handles of Power*. The chapters faced a series of life problems having to do with banishing fear, untangling human relations, shifting the load, overcoming evil, the attainment of radiance of personality and many others. Each chapter contained some great affirmations of faith, a psychologically sound spiritual technique for appropriating spiritual power.

That little book has traveled the world. Thousands of letters have come to my desk from ministers and laymen of all denominations expressing their gratitude for the Silent Communion method it advanced for bringing into manifestation the deepest longings of their hearts.

I am deeply indebted to the Unity School of Christianity at Lee's Summit, Missouri, for my discovery of the great affirmations that work such wonders in human lives. As I was making my pastoral calls among the members of the congregation of the Endion Methodist Church in Duluth, I observed that a large number of them were regular readers of various Unity publications. They were convinced that they received more concrete help from the use of these great affirmations of faith than from any other source. I noted that they were among the most poised, integrated, and well balanced people in my parish. So, I took samples of the literature home with me for careful study. I then went to Kansas City and met the leaders of the Unity movement, including those two remarkable men, Charles and Lowell Fillmore. As I sat at lunch one day with Charles Fillmore, I was amazed to learn that he was ninety years of age, though he looked and acted like a man twenty-five years younger. The very next day he was to start on a long drive to California, and he told me that he would stop here and there en route to deliver lectures on the Unity movement. When I learned that both he and his wife, Myrtle Fillmore, had been near death's door with fatal diseases half a century before that date, I knew that he had possession of a secret of healing power that few people know anything about.

I went through their giant institution and talked with many of the 500 employees. I was present when every wheel stopped in their huge printing establishment for all the workers to bow their heads in two minutes of silent prayer which was concluded by an affirmation of faith coming over a loud-speaker, so that all could join in making this statement of faith their own. I found a peace and harmony among these people that I had observed nowhere else. When we stopped at the large file that contains the names of tens of thousands of individuals across the world who have received help from Unity publications, I took a look at the card of Starr Daily. I had read his book, *Love Can Open Prison Doors*, and I already knew what a spritual power this man had become through his writings and his lectures. How surprised I was to learn that when he first read a Unity publication he was a sour, disgruntled prisoner in a state institution! His use of the Silent Communion technique and of his absolute faith in the power of God had really opened prison doors and started him on a career of spiritual helpfulness that is almost without parallel in the annals of religious literature. Starr Daily is only one of the tens of thousands whose lives have been healed and integrated through the Unity movement in the last half-century. These people had the "how" of applied Christianity that I had been seeking. They had something that worked! It solved problems. It ennobled and beautified life. I was not surprised to learn that they had built up a constituency of more than two million souls in all countries of the world, and that they had done so through love offerings alone and not through high-powered campaigns for gifts of money. One of the things that I especially like about the Unity movement is that they never urge their followers to leave their own churches. Quite the contrary. They always suggest that the followers remain loyal members of their respective churches and work within them to bring greater health, peace, and harmony to all members.

I returned to Duluth and worked out a series of sermons that finally found their way into *Handles of Power.* All our people began an intensive test of this practical method of appropriating the riches of the Kingdom of Heaven that is within us. Wonderful things began to happen to all of us.

On a Sunday afternoon one of our well known businessmen came to see me at my home. He was greatly troubled about his lovely daughter. The business concern for which she was working had promoted her to an important position that required her to answer the telephone all day and to quote prices for certain complicated services. She was not doing well in the new job, was making costly mistakes, and the company had threatened her with dismissal unless she could improve rapidly. She could not sleep nor eat, and her father was afraid of a nervous breakdown.

I asked him to have his daughter come right out. She told her story simply—her haunting fear that she would make mistakes, the way her heart pounded whenever the telephone rang, and finally her despair whenever she thought of the disgrace of being sacked for inefficiency. It was perfectly clear to me what was happening. Her vivid picture of failure, dwelt upon tenaciously night and day, was rapidly bringing about her undoing. So I explained carefully the relation of the conscious to the unconscious mind and the creative power of every thought—for good or ill. Then I drew for her a vivid picture of herself as God's agent working with and for him, of the friendly people on the other end of the telephone each time it rang, asking for the information she knew so well how to give. I finally drew a mental portrait of her friendly employer becoming perfectly delighted with her work and commending her for its excellence. Then I went to my study and brought back a series of Silent Communion cards full of the kind of affirmations that she needed. She was instructed to concentrate on holding the new picture in the center of consciousness as she repeated, slowly and meaningfully, the affirmations that linked the whole venture with God.

I didn't see her again for several months. Then one day when I finished addressing a group of working girls she followed me down the hall. One look at her radiant face, and I knew what had happened. "It worked—beautifully," she said. "One week after our interview my boss came to me and said: 'What on earth happened to you about a week ago? You aren't the same girl any more. And the mistakes have vanished into nothingness.' " That evening I saw her father in his place of business. With a slow shake of the head and with deep conviction, he said: "All the money in the world wouldn't be enough to settle accounts for what you did for my daughter. It changed her whole life." I hastened to assure him that I had not made the change. I had merely painted a vivid picture and helped her transfer it to her own power generator in the mind and soul. God had done the rest.

I have been in the First Methodist Church of Iowa City for eleven years, applying the technique of affirmation consistently, and have seen the morning attendance grow from an average of 400 to more than 2,000 in two identical services of worship each Sunday morning. People are spiritually hungry. They want to be told very specifically *how* to appropriate spiritual power; *how* to lay hold of the inexhaustible riches of Christ. This technique is the "*how.*"

That is why we have returned to the use of the Silent Communion method in this book. The remarkable results obtained and demonstrated by many thousands of people with haunting human needs can be yours, dear reader friend, if you will pay the price of *diligence* and *absolute persistence*.

L. L. Dunnington

Contents

The Use of the Silent Communion Affirmations

Read the first chapter through slowly with careful attention to the last pages where the relationship of the conscious to the unconscious mind is discussed. That and all subsequent chapters close with great affirmations. *Observe a few moments of silence at the beginning and end of the day, and as often through the day as possible, repeating slowly and meaningfully these affirmatives. They will thus sink into the unconscious mind where God can use them to heal and integrate body, mind and affairs.*

Thus, you will be able so to fill your mind with positive thoughts of the faith, hope, love variety that there will be no lodgment available for fear, worry, hatred or jealousy. *You can win through if you truly desire it!*

THE INNER SPLENDOR

CHAPTER ONE

The Inner Splendor

A number of years ago, I read something from Angela Morgan that stirred me to the depths. Its haunting and thrilling truth has kept returning to my mind ever since. Here it is:

I am aware,
As I go commonly sweeping the stair,
Doing my part of the everyday care—
Human and simple my lot and my share—
  I am aware of a marvelous thing:
  Voices that murmur and ethers that ring
  In the far stellar spaces wherein cherubim sing.
I am aware of a passion that pours
Down channels of fire through Infinity's doors;
  Forces terrific, with melody shod,
  Music that mates with the pulses of God.
I am aware of the glory that runs
From the core of myself to the core of the suns . . .
I am aware of the splendor that ties
All the things of the earth with the things of the skies.

If you react to these lines as I did, you have already read them two or three times before proceeding. And you have probably said to yourself: "She is right. There is a splendor deep within me also which is quickened into life when I glimpse beauty and truth and goodness in God's wonderful universe."

Your acknowledgment will, in all probability, be followed by a most disturbing realization that *this glorious splendor lies imprisoned within us most of the time.* Fear, worry, avarice, envy, and feelings of inferiority take over the citadel of consciousness, and "the splendor that ties all the things of the earth with the things of the skies" becomes smothered.

We can thank God that the splendor within Angela Morgan was not to be denied expression just because certain editors were blind to the truth and beauty of her lines. She was young and totally unknown when she wrote them, and so she received so many rejection slips that she was tempted to give up hope of finding a publisher.

This is the way she told her story to Dr. W. L. Stidger:

"One day an inspiration came to me. I would go to Mark Twain and see if he wouldn't help me. So one hot summer day I started for Stormfield, in Connecticut. I got off at a little way station three miles from Stormfield and walked down a dusty road. My shoes were full of dust, I was wet with sweat and my hair disheveled. But when I got in sight of Stormfield I stopped dead still in the middle of that dusty road, looked up into the blazing sun and prayed a little prayer: 'Now you Power of the universe that is back of that sun. You can do anything, and I want you to help me get Mr. Clemens to read my poem.'

"I went up to that house full of confidence. I walked up the steps and rang the bell. Mark Twain came to the door, looked at me, smiled, and invited me to come in. I was never able to determine whether that smile was one of amusement at my looks after that three mile tramp in the heat and dust or what it was. He himself was immaculately dressed in a white summer suit. We went in and he read the poem over and then said, 'We'll have lunch first, and then you can read it to me yourself.'

"My heart jumped a beat. But pretty soon I found myself sitting on the porch with Mark Twain and Albert Bigelow Paine, his biographer, eating lunch. The only thing I can remember about that lunch was that Mr. Clemens spent most of the time swatting flies. Now and then he would kill one on Mr. Paine's head. After lunch he said, 'Now we are to hear the poem.'

"It was like a command performance and I arose to it as best I could, summoning to my help that something inside of me I had been taught was there for all emergencies.

"When I had finished reading that poem Mark Twain turned to Mr. Paine and said: 'I'm very glad! I'm very glad the Lord made her. I don't always approve of his handiwork but this time I do. And this poem must be published, Paine. You send it to the editor of *Collier's Weekly* and tell him that if he has any sense he will publish this poem.'

"And Mark Twain in that kind act of encouragement also released something inside of me and gave me my chance, a good deed for which I have always been grateful to his memory.

"All of us have this imprisoned splendor within us. We are like the power in an atom about which they are always talking in scientific circles these days. They talk to me in learned terms of a split electron and I do not know what they mean from a technical point of view; but I know what they mean when they talk of a hidden power, *an imprisoned splendor in human beings.*" *

Jesus put this glorious truth much more simply when he said, "The kingdom of heaven is within you"! We have all heard those magic words hundreds of times, so often in fact that their terrific impact escapes us. The kingdom of heaven? The realm of love and poise and understanding and creativity within *us*? The splendor of God himself with all its cleansing, healing power? The answer is *Yes, it is there!* That is exactly what Jesus said and meant.

Little children have it. How spontaneously they react to the simplest things! How fully and completely they live some of the shining hours of childhood! Then their elders go to work to get them to conform to the cynical, joyless, competitive, negative world of adults, and gradually they lose the lovely thing which was their heritage at birth.

Join Jesus's disciples for a moment, and listen intently. They asked: "Who is the greatest in the kingdom of heaven?" Some little children were playing near by, and Jesus called one of them to him and placed him in the very

* W. L. Stidger, *There Are Sermons in Stories* (Nashville, Tenn.: Abingdon-Cokesbury Press, 1942), pp. 106–107.

center of the group and said: "Verily I say unto you, Except ye be converted, and become as little children, ye shall not enter into the kingdom of heaven. Whosoever therefore shall humble himself as this little child, the same is greatest in the kingdom of heaven. And whoso shall receive one such little child in my name receiveth me." (Matt. 18:3–5.)

Children possess imagining power in remarkable degree. In their games they can become fathers or mothers or engineers or policemen or truck drivers or generals in a second of time. Their active imaginations can work the miracle of transformation so instantaneously as to astound their dull, sober elders. They are humble and teachable. Above all, they possess astounding faith.

These are the things Jesus is talking about as he sets a little child in the midst of his inquiring disciples. The glorious splendor of the kingdom of heaven that is within us can be released only as we give rein to imagination and have faith to believe that we are made in the image of God, that we too possess creative power, that we can reflect love and understanding and forgiveness and graciousness even to our enemies. And when we dare to act *as if* these things are true for us they become true. But we can never enter the kingdom of heaven, we can never release the imprisoned splendor, until we demonstrate the humility, faith, and imagining power of little children.

It was this truth that lay back of the healing power of Jesus. After he had gained a sick man's confidence, he could lay his gentle, strong, sure hands upon him and send the healing power of God coursing through his veins. So could the disciples when they fasted and prayed, and rid themselves of doubt and fear. Jesus promised them and all other followers of his that they could do these things and even greater. But, alas, and alas, his church has largely lost such healing power because it no longer believes.

I have recently read *Everyman's Search*, by Dr. Rebecca Beard. Dr. Beard practiced medicine for some years, albeit with a haunting feeling that there was a healing power available that was more potent than drugs. She realized that every physical body, properly nourished, had within it disease-fighting powers that should be sufficient to return most ill persons to health, especially if the mind were filled with faith, hope, and love.

One day Dr. Beard suffered a heart attack. Her friends said, "You must put your affairs in order, for you cannot live through another heart attack." She tells us that that signal sent her to her knees, literally and figuratively, with a cry from her heart to her Heavenly Father to "either take it from me or take me."

There followed a great spiritual illumination and healing. She instinctively knew at that moment that the rest of her life would have to be spent helping others to find healing. She stopped administering drugs. She says she had nothing against the judicious use of drugs by other doctors, but had found something better. She used vitamins and hormones to build up her patients physically, but the most important thing she did was to try to give them faith and confidence in the simple fact that God does all the healing anyway, either with or without drugs. She told her patients how to rid their minds and hearts of fear, worry, hatred, and jealousy—negative thoughts that produce disease. On the positive side she taught them how to keep the mind tuned in to love, understanding, forgiveness, and joy as found in Christ and confidently to expect healing of all the hurt places of body, mind, and spirit. She has had remarkable results.

She quotes the testimony of Albert E. Cliffe, famous Canadian chemist, in his book, *Lessons in Living:*

"As a food chemist, I know that the foods I eat each day are converted into the various parts of my body; in other words, my physical well-being depends for its development upon my daily diet. However, several years ago it was found that in spite of a so-called perfect diet of the right foods, many people suffered from disease, which according to the principles of nutrition should never have occurred.

"It was then that I came into my study of the mind, which has taught me that the food I give to my mind each hour and each day is of far greater importance than the food I give to my stomach. The words of Jesus in this respect are most applicable, 'Be not therefore anxious, saying, What shall we eat? or, What shall we drink?' By an application of His words I discovered that I alone was the cause of my intense suffering from stomach ulcers for twenty-seven years. Once I proved that my mental vitamins were the real source of my sickness or health, I became as I wished to become, healthy, happy and successful."

But it seems to have been the remarkable case of Alice Newton of Leavenworth, Kansas, that gave Dr. Beard her greatest confidence in the early days of her healing ministry. A chronic constitutional affliction had left Mrs. Newton's body emaciated and her abdomen three times its normal size. She had had four doctors in Kansas City and St. Louis who could do nothing for her. As a last resort, she came to Dr. Beard and asked, "Do you think that I can be healed by prayer and nothing else?"

Dr. Beard admits that she was a bit dubious way down deep inside but quickly replied in the affirmative. Mrs. Newton then stoutly asserted her own belief that it could be done and promptly mapped out a strict regime involving unquestioning belief and prayer which she would follow every day as long as necessary.

For two years she prayed and waited and never lost faith. Her doctor came often to examine her and to suggest from time to time that he be allowed to tap her abdomen, but she was now determined to rely completely on God's healing power.

Then, one night it happened. She had a vivid dream of the crucifixion of Christ. She saw them thrust a spear into his side and, since she seemed to be standing near the cross, she thought she put her hand out to shield him from the thrust. At that moment she awakened to find her hand resting on her own abdomen, but it was flat and normal. She knew she had been healed. The scales the next morning revealed the fact that she had lost thirty-eight and a half pounds in one night. The doctor was greatly excited when he came and asked again and again: "What came away? Where did it go?" Mrs. Newton could only answer: "Nothing came away—no water—nothing. I was instantly healed, and lost thirty-eight and a half pounds of my old illness."

All day long friends and neighbors filed through the house to see for themselves. The Leavenworth *Times* sent a reporter and published his story January 13, 1939. When Dr. Beard wrote that the Leavenworth *Times* had mentioned this healing every year on the anniversary of the healing, I wrote to Mrs. Newton and asked for confirmation. She sent me, by registered mail, a copy of the paper that carried the original story and also a copy of the *Times* for January 13, 1951, which reviewed the story and reported Mrs. Newton as hale and hearty and radiant. She also wrote me a beautiful letter of confirmation.

What happened to Mrs. Newton is happening to hundreds of others. Paul said: "Know ye not that your body is the temple of the Holy Ghost which is in you, which ye have of God?" (I Cor. 6:19). Let us stop a moment and think about that. My body and yours are the home of the Holy Spirit which is God! They are the home of Supreme Intelligence, Love, Poise, Health, and Healing Power. This is the Splendor of God, but it is, for most of us, an imprisoned splendor—imprisoned by fear, envy, anxiety, anger, hatred, jealousy and resentment, and a whole host of negative, health-destroying thoughts.

The greatest single problem that any of us faces, therefore, is finding a technique of spiritual power that will turn the mind away from these destructive emotions toward the radiance and love of God. This process then frees the imprisoned splendor which is always present deep within us awaiting release. As Jesus said, the kingdom of heaven *is* within us; but it can be released only by faith. Again and again, when Jesus healed, he said, "*According to thy faith be it done unto thee.*"

That, dear reader friends, is what this entire book is about, the discovery and use of the technique that will release the imprisoned splendor that Jesus said *is within us. Only about a tenth of the mind is conscious, with power to think and reason and judge. The other nine-tenths is unconscious, with no power to reason, but so constructed that it must accept at face value what the conscious mind dwells upon and try to bring that, good or bad, positive or negative, into manifestation.*

Every thought, therefore, is creative for good or ill. If we train ourselves to dwell upon what is true and good and beautiful, if we have the single eye of faith, hope, and love to the exclusion of all else, these thoughts will flavor and dominate the deep well of the unconscious and result in happy, poised, integrated personalities. This is the law of mind and the way of faith. Conversely, if we allow thoughts of discontent, anger, envy, fear, jealousy, and hatred to occupy a large portion of our waking hours, we shall most assuredly become weak, sour, fear-ridden, diseased souls shunned by all, loved by none. "As a man thinketh in his heart (unconscious mind), *so is he." All of Jesus's teaching is based upon this law of mind and spirit.*

That is why we shall close each chapter of this book with some powerful affirmations—techniques for appropriating spiritual power, poise, health of body, mind and affairs. You are urged to repeat these affirmations many times a day, the first thing in the morning, the last thing at night before trailing off into slumber. Say them slowly, meaningfully, and with deep conviction, and *keep at it.* The results will be as remarkable for you as they have been for thousands of others who have read my previous books containing this same simple technique.

Silent Communion for Recognizing the Kingdom of God Within

Jesus said, "The kingdom of God is within you" (Luke 17:21).

The kingdom of God is, therefore, within me. Infinite possibilities for the growth and unfoldment of health, harmony, and peace are mine NOW as I resolve to dwell exclusively in the realm of faith, hope, and love.

CHAPTER TWO

The Inner Splendor Released

Without apology for the repetition, let us briefly summarize the vital truth with which the first chapter closed; for, unless our readers fully comprehend these incontrovertible facts, much of what our book has to say cannot be understood nor utilized in rechanneling the life forces toward greater health and harmony of body, mind, and affairs.

Jesus is speaking: "A good man out of the good treasure of his heart bringeth forth that which is good; and an evil man out of the evil treasure of his heart bringeth forth that which is evil: for of the abundance of the heart his mouth speaketh." (Luke 6:45.)

Let us note first of all that Jesus, when he speaks of the heart, is not referring to our blood pump. He is speaking of the deep or unconscious mind. Psychologists tell us that approximately a tenth of the human mind is conscious while the other nine-tenths is unconscious. The conscious mind can think and reason. The unconscious part of the mind is a vast repository of thoughts of the conscious mind which have been received uncritically, for the unconscious cannot think or reason. If the critical or conscious mind is allowed to dwell at great length upon fear, hatred, envy, or jealousy, those negative emotions sink into the deeper mind, which in turn must bring them into manifestation in body and spirit.

On the other hand, if the conscious mind is so trained as to dwell only upon faith and hope and love, if a man visualizes health and confidence and poise, those positive virtues likewise sink into the "heart" and must in turn be brought into manifestation. It is the law of mind and body, which are bound together in the bundle of life. Now, read Jesus's words again: "*A good man out of the good treasure of his heart bringeth forth that which is good; and an evil man out of the evil treasure of his heart bringeth forth that which is evil.*" Do you see more clearly what he is talking about?

Long held resentment is now believed to be a common cause of hives. Doctors at New York Hospital–Cornell University Medical College have been experimenting along this very line. Thirty patients who had periodic attacks of the blotchy, itchy skin disorder called hives were picked at random and told to eat what they pleased. Their life histories were carefully taken, with special attention to the emotional circumstances in which the attacks occurred.

The investigators found that they could cause the skin to flare up in most cases merely by discussing the personal problem to which the subject had a strong emotional response. Strangely, the response was never hostility, grief, or anxiety. It was, in every case, resentment—each patient saw himself as the victim of unjust treatment about which he could do nothing.

When a patient's resentment was thus aroused delicate instruments attached to his body showed a dilation of minute blood vessels in the skin, bringing on hives. Family, marital, and business situations were involved, but all had this in common: the individual in every case was "taking a beating" under circumstances which would not permit him to fight back or run away.

The *British Medical Journal* once contained this statement: "The truth is that no cell in the human body can ever be removed completely from the power of spirit." Spirit, whether positive or negative, is generated by thought. Words are symbols of thought. That explains the meaning of John 15:7: "If ye abide in me, and my *words* abide in you, ye shall ask what ye will, and it shall be done unto you." Let a man stay tuned in continuously to thoughts of peace, serenity, truth, love, and joy as found in the very heart of God, and his deep mind or "heart" will accumulate a treasure which must be brought into manifestation. Every cell in the body will be bathed with healing power.

There is a new word upon our medical horizon these days. It is the word "psychosomatic," applied to medicine—psychosomatic medicine, subject and subtitle of Dr. Flanders Dunbar's wonderful book *Mind and Body*. The word is derived from the Greek *psyche*—which has been translated as mind or spirit or soul, but which actually includes all of them—and *soma*, body. The medical fraternity has concluded that body and mind are an inseparable unit, and that a sick mind and spirit cause most of the illnesses of the human body. Dr. Dunbar in her Foreword makes the startling estimate that four-fifths of our population need the services of an expert in psychosomatic medicine.

Dr. Carl Binger in *The Doctor's Job* speaks about "splinters in the soul." He says more people are sick because they are unhappy than are unhappy because they are sick. The cause of most of our illnesses is within us, and the cure is within us, too. The Mayo Clinic states that, of 15,000 ulcer patients, four-fifths were found not to have any physical cause for ulcer of the stomach. Four out of five were suffering from emotional disturbance. That is why ulcers of the stomach have come to be known as the "wound stripe of civilization."

Perhaps that explains the definite trend today back toward churches that are preaching the whole gospel of Christ with special emphasis upon the good news of the healing power of Christ. The busy, hurrying, uncertain life of our day is causing millions to go to pieces emotionally. An emotional debacle is soon followed by a physical crack-up. The Sermon on the Mount is the only blueprint ever given to man that can and will give him health and peace in the midst of confusion and death.

Miracles of healing happen every week at old St. Stephen's Episcopal Church in Philadelphia under the dynamic ministry of Dr. Alfred W. Price. Read his thrilling testimony in the *Churchman* for October 15, 1951:

"We have been practicing what we would like to call sane Christian healing in St. Stephen's Church, Philadelphia, for the past nine years. We have set aside one day a week in an endeavor, on the one hand, not to over-emphasize the healing ministry, and on the other hand, to do justice to the clear command of our Lord to 'heal the sick.' Doctors and psychiatrists send patients to us and some doctors even sit in the pews with their patients. Hundreds of cures of organic, functional and mental disease have been attested by laboratory and X-ray tests from colds to cancer, from arthritis to chronic alcoholism, from ear-ache to epilepsy, from mental depression to mental derangement. We have discovered from our experience over the years that there is no disease that is incurable, and no problem that cannot be solved when God is allowed to 'take over.'

"Does this sound like magic? Perhaps the reader at this point will rebel and refuse to accept this evidence. Perhaps he will share the conviction of many good people that spiritual healing sounds like a cheap and easy way out of one's troubles and therefore there cannot be much in it. Many people see in spiritual healing the danger of hysterical and exaggerated concern for merely physical health. Many more shy away because they feel that sickness and disease are sent from God as a punishment for wrongdoing, and therefore it is wrong to pray for healing.

"There is nothing cheap or easy in fulfilling the essential conditions upon which healing depends. Absolute relinquishment of self and personal ambition is not easy. The elimination of all reservations, wrong motives, all self-interest is not easy. It is not easy to lose one's resentment; it is not easy to confess our sins to God and accept His forgiveness; it is not easy to make thankfulness a constant habit of our minds, but that is what is required in order to create the proper conditions for spiritual healing. Yes, it is difficult but not impossible. I have seen people go all out in these matters, and, as a consequence, have had such a wonderful inner release that the healing power of God rushed in with the force of a Niagara river and literally re-created every cell, every tissue, every organ, the whole personality, body, mind and spirit.

"The writer is convinced that God is on the side of health and against disease. He has implanted within each one of us marvelous remedial and healing agencies. He has implanted within us the mechanism to solve every problem, every difficulty, every circumstance that may come to us in our lifetime. These agencies must be released. They are locked up within us. 'The kingdom of God is within you,' said Jesus. All the healing agencies are buried within us, waiting to be released. This is the heart of the Gospel that the power of the Holy Spirit is within us, to heal, to inspire, and to give life, but it has become the neglected part of our religion. We forget that God is not only outside us, but He is also within us. 'The Spirit of Truth abideth with you and shall be in you.'

"I believe in this power with my whole heart. I have seen it work and can humbly say that God has allowed me to share in bringing this miracle of health to others. You, too, may share it if you will fulfill the conditions, which I frankly admit are not easy for most of us brought up and conditioned in a materialistic and spiritually limited environment. God wants us to be well and happy. That is the way He planned Life. If our faith and trust are pure, our love uncontaminated, our prayer constant and without any taint of selfishness, our Father is eager to heal us of our diseases. The Christian ideal is a God-filled personality, not for health's sake, but for God's sake, and for the sake of our fellowmen."

At these Thursday meetings, Dr. Price preaches a simple faith-filled sermon based on New Testament promises. Then he turns his back on the people, faces the altar, and prays:

"O Lord, take my mind and think through it. Take my heart and set it on fire with love. Take these hands and through them bring to these, thy suffering children, the fullness of thy healing power. Amen."

After the prayer, those sick of heart, mind, and body make their way to the altar. Many faces are harassed and sad. Some hobble along on crutches. There is an awe-inspiring silence as the tall man of God places his hands on each one and prays:

"May the mercy of God and the love of our Lord Jesus Christ and the power of his Holy Spirit, which are here now, enter your soul, your mind and your body for healing. Amen."

Typical of the letters of testimony that come daily to Dr. Price's desk is this one:

"Before I leave for my home in Watertown, Mass., I want to tell you of the marvelous cure that happened to me at the altar of your church.

"I came to Philadelphia to inspect the records of the branch office of the concern which employed me. I was staying at the ——— Hotel and contracted a fungus growth on my right leg. It grew steadily worse and my leg from the ankle to the knee was a mass of running sores. Gangrene set in and the doctor despaired of saving it. It looked like a sure amputation.

"Alone in the city and panic stricken, I happened to see the sign in front of your church calling attention to the Healing service. I was on my way at the time to Jefferson Hospital where the doctor had engaged a room for me. It was close to 5:30 p.m. and I entered St. Stephen's Church. I listened to your address on healing. Your words seemed to reach my inner consciousness and led me to come forward in faith with the others to receive the laying on of hands. I cannot describe the feeling that came over me. I seemed to receive immediate healing.

"I walked away without the help of my cane. I continued my journey to the hospital and the next morning when the bandages were removed the surgeon noted with amazement the improved condition. In two days I was discharged as completely cured.

"I have been a lifelong member of the Episcopal Church

but I have never known about this work of spiritual healing until by chance I came into your church."

Dr. Price explains his healing work thus: "Spiritual healing, we are convinced, is based on solid foundation of the Holy Scriptures, sound science, psychology, and common sense. The basic principle on which we operate is that man is a unit of body, mind, and spirit. Any malady that affects one part of that unity affects the whole."

I personally like Dr. Price's sane attitude. He says doctors often come with their patients and sit in the pews through a service. I like the saneness of a doctor who realizes that drugs alone are insufficient to heal a body when the root cause of the illness is psychic or spiritual. I therefore think that the best approach to illness is to accept all the help a good doctor can give plus all the help God can give through our faith in his healing power. I see no reason to assume that going to a good doctor implies a lack of faith in God. A great physician often brings confidence and hope to the sick by his very presence because of the years of arduous preparation he has put in to make himself an expert. The patient should then be in an excellent position to go on from there, to concentrate on the healing power of the Great Physician and to cause every cell of his pain-racked body to be bathed in healing power.

Silent Communion for Healing Power

"For I am the Lord that healeth thee" (Exodus 15:62).

The forgiveness, mercy, and love of the Holy Spirit is flooding my soul and every cell of my body at this moment, releasing the healing power of the kingdom of heaven that is within me.

CHAPTER THREE

A Crystal-Clear Spring

Jesus in his conversation with the woman at the well (John 4:5–24) spoke these matchless words: "Whosoever drinketh of this water shall thirst again: But whosoever drinketh of the water that I shall give him shall never thirst; but the water that I shall give him shall be in him a well of water springing up into everlasting life." What musical and meaningful words in a parched land where crystal-clear well water, continuously springing from inexhaustible depths, was a matter of life and death!

His reference, of course, is to the human soul. When the kingdom of heaven which is within us is not clogged by fear, worry, resentment, lust, envy, and greed, it springs up out of the depths in loving words and acts of beauty and harmony that bless the world. When the heart is clogged with emotional debris, it must be cleaned out before the clear spring water can flow again. The only way to accomplish the desired result is to pray for Almighty God to forgive us our sins, to clear out the depraved depths of our burdened hearts or unconscious minds so that his well of spirit-water may spring up in words and deeds full of the love and understanding of an outgoing self.

Anne Byrd Payson, wealthy eastern socialite, was "fashionable, fleshy, and futile," according to her own testimony, until she was sixty years old. She lived on the surface of life but with a gnawing thirst for the pure upspringing water of life. Then came her "shining hour," and all life was suddenly changed. She tells us that she found Dr. E. Stanley Jones's book, *The Christ of the Indian Road*, on her reading table by her bed one night and reluctantly picked it up because nothing more interesting was at hand. It soon had her spellbound, however, and she read on into the night. A deep hunger for the certain knowledge of the inner presence of God stirred within her as she finally arose and gazed from her bedroom window upon a world of darkness. She writes:

"It was then that Christ's presence shone within me—I knew myself to be a thought in his mind. No sight or sound announced it, no vision and no voice; but a bright hour rose from the wet and dark of the sleeping city. In a new sense of protection I dared face thoughts from which I habitually ran away and dared review tragedies by the light of a defined and increasing radiance. When the first stirrings of the household came and I went back to bed, I prayed; prayed that I might never forget or vulgarize that lovely hour." *

Anne Byrd Payson had experienced conversion, or a

* Anne Byrd Payson, *I Follow the Road* (Nashville, Tenn.: Abingdon-Cokesbury Press, 1933), p. 36.

reorientation of her life away from self toward God and the service of mankind. The completeness of the change becomes crystal-clear as one reads her two remarkable books, *I Follow the Road* and *Rule of the Road.* Conversion, as Dr. Jones says, is really the gradual or sudden changing from the Kingdom of Self to the Kingdom of God through the power of Christ. To some it comes gradually, but to others suddenly.

Under our modern pressures each of us reverses the order of Jesus's command to seek first the kingdom of heaven. No, sir! We are wiser than that. We seek first the wealth of the world. We say we must be assured of food and shelter and clothes and a good bank account. The pattern we follow is of competition and aggression, of cleverness in self-promotion until, in Channing Pollock's searing phrase, "the world's slow stain" tarnishes our former brightness. Slowly the realization dawns that many of the rich and powerful people we have tried to emulate are the most unhappy and sad of all. They are all too often least in the kingdom of peace.

Then comes a moment of stabbing awareness. We may be reading a book or talking to a spiritual friend or viewing a quiet sunset when suddenly, from out of the depths, God speaks to us in a still, small voice. We know that worry, weariness, and frustration are never cast out by the possession of external things or by money and high position.

It is at such a moment that the soul instinctively cries out for the forgiveness and peace of God, and our own "shining hour" becomes a reality.

In the New Birth, this is what happens as nearly as one can describe it. The great well of the unconscious mind or heart has been taking to itself the sins, doubts, fears, worries, frustrations, and complexes that the conscious mind has been dwelling upon. The load grows heavier and heavier. Comes then a flash of illumination of what life could be like if we were to surrender to Christ's way. The weary and burdened soul reaches blindly but confidently out after God through his *daring faith that there is a God who hears and forgives and loves.* He experiences, either suddenly or gradually, a great relief. The burden is gone, and in its place is "a well-defined radiance."

Psychologists tell us that this new peace of mind and soul has been caused by a *transfer* of the heart's burden to God. The man is free. The stream of his consciousness is no longer inward toward self but outward toward God and man. He has ceased to be interested primarily in the things of the world. He begins to seek first the things of the spirit, the kingdom of heaven. New dignity and meaning and worth come welling up from within. This is indeed the well of water, clear as crystal, springing up into everlasting life.

It is good to live a good, moral life and follow the Golden Rule, and America and the whole world need more people who will do so. But let it be said at once that following the Golden Rule is not enough to feed the flowing well of water that springs up into everlasting life. A good, moral life needs one thing more: complete self-surrender to the Living God including frequent daily communion with the Source of our being and reliance on Him for health, strength, and guidance in all humility.

One of the most instructive books along this line that I have read in many a day is the autobiography *Fifty Years with the Golden Rule.* In it J. C. Penney tells us that his first lesson with the Golden Rule came early. As a small lad, he had planted a field of watermelons that grew into a bountiful crop. At fair time he borrowed a horse and wagon, drove to a spot just outside the entrance to the grounds, and started hawking his juicy, succulent product. Melons were being sold at a furious rate when he spied his frowning father on the outskirts of the crowd. "Pick up and go home. You're a disgrace to the Penneys," said the stern parent.

Little Jim Penney was crestfallen and hurt. When his father came home, he explained that the people selling things inside the fair grounds had bought "concessions" and paid good money for the right to sell; that Jim, in setting up shop outside the grounds, had taken unfair advantage of a brother and had violated the Golden Rule of Jesus. Little Jim got the point. In fact, he got it in such a way that he was emotionally conditioned by the experience for the rest of his life.

"Once again," he writes, "in his direct, unadorned way, my father had instilled in me a point of honor which, as time went on, revealed itself to me in the form of a foundation stone of human dealing in the business world. Money is important; but the practice of the Golden Rule in making money—as in every other aspect of human relations—is the most substantial asset of civilized man." *

As a matter of fact, Mr. Penney went on to establish a chain of more than a thousand stores bearing his name from coast to coast. He made a fabulous fortune and made his name a household word throughout the country. Here are the six principles that guided his every step: (1) Preparation wins—know your business thoroughly. (2) Hard work wins. (3) Honesty wins. (4) Confidence in men wins. (He developed honest, hard-working, capable men within his stores and then trusted them as managers and partners.) (5) The spirit wins—the spirit of the pioneers which solves problems and conquers difficulties. (6) A practical application of the Golden Rule wins. "Therefore all things whatsoever ye would that men should do to you, do ye even so to them; for this is the law and the prophets."

On these solid, ethical and moral foundation stones, Mr. Penney not only made a huge fortune but gave millions away to such Christian enterprises as the Memorial Home Community (the Penney Farms), the National Youth Radio Conference, and the *Christian Herald*. Yes, he was a big man; but, as he says, he had grown big in his own mind, too.

Then came the crash of 1929. At first it did not bother

* J. C. Penney, *Fifty Years with the Golden Rule* (New York: Harper & Brothers, 1950), p. 25.

him. He borrowed millions to keep his benevolent enterprises afloat. Down and down went the American economy until, in 1930, J. C. Penney was flat broke. His wife let all their servants go and began doing her own housework. Lawsuits were filed against him as head of the Penney stores, and bitterness engulfed the great man's spirit.

Still, he was not a man to run. He fought on and gradually made a comeback; but something was wrong. Shingles broke out over one whole side of his body. He became a walking shadow of his former self. His physical strength was gone. He could not sleep without a sedative.

One night in the Kellogg sanitarium at Battle Creek, Michigan, he felt he was going to die before morning. He got weakly out of bed and wrote several farewell letters, sealed them, turned out the light, and fell into what he thought was his last sleep. In the morning, however, he was still alive; so he got up, dressed and shuffled downstairs.

Stealing along a corridor, he heard the strains of an old familiar hymn:

> "Be not dismayed whate'er betide,
> God will take care of you . . . "

He moved slowly toward the chapel. The music grew louder:

> "All you may need He will provide,
> God will take care of you . . .
> Lonely and sad, from friends apart . . .
> No matter what may be the test,
> God will take care of you."

As he sank into a rear seat, he heard:

> "Lean, weary one, upon His breast,
> God will take care of you."

Somebody was reading the Scripture: "Come unto me, all ye that labour and are heavy laden, and I will give you rest." Suddenly up went an agonizing prayer from the very bottom of his heart: "Lord, I can do nothing. Will you take care of me?"

Now, let Mr. Penney tell it: "In the next few moments something happened to me . . . I had a feeling of being lifted out of an immensity of dark space into a spaciousness of warm and brilliant sunlight . . . God with His boundless and matchlessly patient love was there to help me . . . A weight lifted from my spirit. I came out of that room a different man, renewed. I had gone in bowed with a paralysis of spirit, utterly adrift. I came forth with a soaring sense of release, from a bondage of gathering death to a pulse of helpful living. I had glimpsed God." *

Mr. Penney goes on to say that the premonition of death that he had had the night before was but the premonition of the death of the man he had been; he had been made ill by wrong thinking, by reliance upon himself instead of upon God, by fear, worry, resentment, and despair.

From the morning of his rebirth, he steadily improved in physical, mental, and spiritual health. New courage and resolution came as the real assets for a new start. Words from the Gospel of Mark took on new meaning for him:

* *Fifty Years with the Golden Rule*, p. 159.

"For what shall it profit a man, if he shall gain the whole world, and lose his own soul?"

Mr. Penney's fascinating story illustrates what we meant when we said that living a good moral life and following the Golden Rule was good but not enough for experiencing the joy of the life abundant. He tells us that through the years he had prayed, but not in any intimate, vital, personal way. He believed in God, but he had never experienced the One who was closer "than breathing, and nearer than hands and feet." His real reliance was upon himself, and when that self was wronged by an unjust lawsuit he harbored bitter resentment. He had grown big in his own mind. The reborn J. C. Penney was no longer a great man in his own mind. His basic security was now in God and God alone: a God with whom he humbly talked many times a day; a God on whom he would forever after cast his burden, and whom he would trust completely to bring him through every difficulty. From that glorious morning in the chapel he knew the meaning of the psalmist: "Commit thy way unto the Lord; trust also in him; and he shall bring it to pass" (Psalm 37:5).

Silent Communion for Reorienting My Life Toward God

"Be not afraid, only believe" (Mark 5:36).

I am not afraid any more. I believe that "underneath are the everlasting arms," and I now confess my sins and give my-

self, in all completeness, into the security of the Arms of God. A well of living water is springing up from within, into everlasting life. This I believe with all my heart. On this solid foundation, I am now abiding in peace.

CHAPTER FOUR

The Guard at the Door

Paul is closing his letter to the people of Philippi: "Goodbye, and the Lord be with you always . . . Have *no anxiety* about anything, but make all your wants known to God in prayer and entreaty, and with thanksgiving. Then, through your union with Christ Jesus, the peace of God, so far above any human thought, *will guard your minds and thoughts.*" (Phil. 4:4–7, Goodspeed translation.)

And just how will the peace of God guard our minds and thoughts? Paul at once gives us the key, for he continues: "Now, brothers, let your minds *dwell* on what is true, what is worthy, what is right, what is pure, what is amiable, what is kindly—on everything that is excellent or praiseworthy . . . Then God who gives peace will be with you." (Phil. 4:8–9, Goodspeed translation.)

Paul's technique is simple. The guard at the door of consciousness consists of keeping the mind so continuously tuned in to hope, health, love, and harmony that no negative, fearful thought has a ghost of a chance of getting by. Flood a room with light, and darkness cannot possibly enter. Turn off the light even for a second, and the darkness will take over.

When the conscious mind is allowed to dwell *only* on the good, the true, and the beautiful, when it envisages only health and harmony, positive, healing forces sink into the deep or unconscious mind, which in turn must bring such thoughts into manifestation. If these positive guards at the door of consciousness are alert to let no negative, fearful, despairing intruders inside, the most marvelous results will be had. That is the law of mind and spirit. It is the way God made us. Even Jesus, in his own home town, could accomplish no mighty works because of his neighbors' unbelief. Self-imposed limitations due to carelessness of the guards at the door constitute our only grounds for failure to live the good life God intends for all of his children.

No more thrilling example of this glorious truth has come to my attention than Lieutenant Commander Edwin Miller Rosenberg.* It is little wonder that the Secretary of the Navy, Dan A. Kimball, said the whole Navy was proud of the epic battle which Rosenberg had waged against imminent death.

Graduated from the Naval Academy a few days after Pearl Harbor, Rosenberg was assigned to the U.S.S. *Omaha* as a junior ensign and saw three years of combat duty. He then went to Dallas, Texas, to take flight training and from there to Pensacola. While running an obstacle race in 1945, he hit his groin and suffered an attack of high fever, nausea, and backache. Later, aboard the aircraft carrier *Rudyerd*

* Reported in the *Reader's Digest*, Nov., 1951.

Bay, he knew he was a very sick man. A few months later, surgeons of the Navy Hospital at Chelsea near Boston removed a malignant tumor from his right side. They then told him their grim discovery. He had a cancer inside a kidney, and they were sure he had only two or three weeks to live. He had better see a lawyer and set his affairs in order, they said.

Young Rosenberg hit the ceiling. He declared that he was not going to die, that he was a man of hope and faith and not in the least afraid he was near the end. "No man should try to assess another's hope," he told the doctor, "until he has heard his prayers." Never once did he discuss his illness in anything but positive terms. He took constant radiation, and he prayed without ceasing.

In three months he surprised everyone by appearing to have won his battle. The X-ray plates showed the cancer had disappeared. Thirty days later, however, another examination disclosed a cancer in his neck. Again radiation and positive, hopeful praying, and the battle seemed won once more. After a lapse of a few weeks an examination discovered still another cancer where the first had been. And the experience was repeated a fourth time with never a sign of fear, or doubt that he and God and the doctors would win.

The thrilling thing about it is that they did. Other naval patients with the same dread disease watched and marveled and asked how he did it. He advised prayer without ceasing. Some of them got well, too.

The big question then was how in the world Lieutenant Commander Rosenberg could get back to active duty aboard a good ship. Everywhere he went among the top brass, he struck a stone wall. His case was unprecedented, they said. It was against the law to restore a cancer patient to active duty. More prayers and more action. One day he met Bourke Hickenlooper in the Senate Chamber during a recess. The Iowa Senator promised to introduce a bill that would enable the remarkable young man to get back aboard a ship. To a Senate Committee Rosenberg stoutly affirmed that, with the Lord's help, he thought he had thirty years of service ahead of him if they would recommend passage of the bill.

It was passed by both Senate and House, and was signed by the President on August 22, 1950. Skipper Rosenberg is in the active service of his country today—one of the most lively and inspiring examples the world has ever seen of the power of unwavering faith to solve even the most vexatious of problems. He kept the guard firmly planted at the door, and no destructive demon of doubt or despair could sneak by!

Now, someone may ask: How in the world could a thing like that happen? Cancer! Healed after it had recurred four times! And why does this not happen more often? It seems to me that it does occur far oftener than most of us think. And it always takes place in the lives of people who learn how to stay tuned to the love, radiance, and healing power of God. Spasmodic prayer is simply not good enough for such results. The guard at the door must be so good that not one little fear or doubt gets through—ever.

Dr. Rebecca Beard meditated long about this glorious marvel. And the oftener I read over her suggestive lines, the more it seems to me she points us to an explanation that satisfies both mind and heart:

"When we hear of a marvelous recovery like that of Dr. George Parkhurst's mother, Genevieve Parkhurst, who had a lump in her breast which the doctor wanted to remove, but who was completely healed through prayer, we feel it is almost incomprehensible. As she prayed alone one day, a terrific pain, like an electric shock, went through the lump and down her arm. When she recovered sufficiently, she put her hand where the lump had been, and there was a hollow place as large as a fist. The lump had disappeared. She graciously allowed me to examine her later and I could find nothing in the tissues or glands that did not seem perfectly normal.

"These things seem almost impossible to believe, yet here are great physicists like de Broglie who has given us an insight into the sub-atomic world in the theory of wave mechanics, and who says that when we go below the atom into the world of the electron, the proton and the neutron, we are entering the world of energy. This is an unseen world, and the laws of that world do not coincide with the laws of matter. This disturbs the physicists. Du Noüy deplores this 'gaping breach in the arrogant edifice of science.' Could it be (and I offer this as a subject of contemplation) that the invisible world of energy back of the atom and upon which the atom depends, is the world of the spirit? Could it be that in our spiritual therapy we generate a flow of divine love and life through our being which touches this world of spiritual energy back of the atoms and causes them to arrange themselves in their original harmonious order, thus changing the molecules in the twinkling of an eye? May it be that as we place our hand in the Great Hand, and open ourselves to the healing light, we touch with our other hand the invisible world behind the atom, and in some hitherto incomprehensible way bring these electrons, protons and neutrons into harmonious relationship with each other, thus immediately, without perceptible passage of time, establish normal relations between the cells of that particular tissue? It is not inconceivable." *

Tom Lashar was doing metallurgical research in a defense plant during the last war. One day a tank of inflammable gas exploded, and Tom became a flaming torch. They rushed him to a hospital and dressed the third-degree burns that covered his face and much of his body. He had been married only four months and he did not want Josie to have to endure a man with a hideously scarred face.

So, he started to pray, "Yea, though I walk through the valley of the shadow of death, I will fear no evil: for thou art with me." He felt greatly relieved as the truth back of the words took a firm grip on his imagination. When Josie

* Beard, *Everyman's Search* (New York: Harper & Brothers—first published, 1950).

arrived the doctor pulled a sheet over his head to hide the extent of his burns and the heavy bandages. As this remarkable little girl of great faith stood gazing at that sheet she recalled something she had once determined would be the right procedure in the face of just such a calamity—*she would make her imagination an ally instead of an enemy.* By having unbounded faith in the power of God to do the seeming impossible, she would deliberately choose to believe that all was well with Tom. Her creative imagining power was shifted into high gear, and she instantly started visualizing her husband as he would be soon—perfectly healed and well.

Walking to the foot of Tom's bed, she reached out and took a firm grip on his feet and began to thank God that his life had been spared, and that he was already on the road to complete recovery without any hideous scars. She prayed aloud, quietly and with a tremor of emotion in her voice that sent a thrill of assurance through Tom so that he joined her in affirming a blessed recovery: "If two of you shall agree on earth as touching any thing that they shall ask, it shall be done for them of my Father which is in heaven." Tom was glad he knew his Bible. Into both their hearts at that moment stole a great peace.

The next day Josie saw Tom without the sheet over his head, and was shocked at what she saw. So was Tom, who demanded a mirror. But Josie had brought the latest picture of her husband, and she rushed to the dresser where it stood, took a good look at it, and began to affirm that that was the way her husband would look again very soon. The doctor had told her that extensive grafting was indicated, and that Tom would be in the hospital two months. Still, these two people of great faith prayed together affirmatively twice a day, and then kept at it most of the rest of the waking day.

In a few days groups of doctors were brought in to observe something that puzzled them. Tom was getting well so fast that skin grafting seemed to be unnecessary after all. And in just fifteen days all the burns were healed, and Tom was dismissed from the hospital.

A miracle? I would not call it that at all. I would say rather that this remarkable case illustrated the outworking of a spiritual law: Tom and Josie kept a guard at the door of consciousness which shut out all doubt and fear while admitting a whole series of visualized mental images of a healed Tom; and to their resolute and joyous affirmations that the love, radiance, and healing power of God were flowing through this sick young man every cell of his body was bound to respond. A miracle is but the outworking of God's laws of spirit on higher levels than man can as yet comprehend.

Silent Communion for Healing Power

God is radiant Light, shining Beauty, contagious Joy, creative Power, all-pervading Love, perfect Understanding, Pur-

ity, Serenity. I am keeping my mind focused so continuously on these things that the peace of God that passes understanding guards my mind and thoughts and brings healing to my body, mind, and spirit.

CHAPTER FIVE

Health from Within

Some time ago, the head of the Massachusetts General Hospital said that more than two-fifths of all the patients it admitted were really not medical but mental and spiritual cases. Their bodily ailments were real and painful enough, but the basic cause of the trouble was uncontrolled emotional conflict of one kind or another. A member of the Mayo Clinic says its doctors can meet the needs of a quarter of the people who come there by the physical instruments of science. But three-quarters of the patients are more difficult because they are passing on the sickness of their minds and souls to their bodies. That requires a different approach.

God made the human body to respond to emotional stimuli and mental suggestions. Anger, jealousy, fear, and hatred cannot be indulged long without seriously affecting every cell in the body. Many diseases are but the prolongation of negative emotional stimuli. On the other hand, thoughts of faith, courage, hope, and love tenaciously held in the presence of God over a long period channel a steady flow of healing power to every cell of the body. As Jesus put it, "By thy words thou shalt be justified, and by thy words thou shalt be condemned." A word is the symbol of the thought we hold, and words are powerful instruments continuously building health or disease.

Two verses in Mark (11:24–25) are worth pondering in this regard. The Master says to his disciples: "Therefore I say unto you, What things soever ye desire, when ye pray, believe that ye receive them, and ye shall have them." Everyone desires a healthy, disease-free body. As we pray for this great boon, we naturally visualize a body aglow with health. By affirming that we already possess it, we generate confidence, harmony, and peace. These healing thoughts, tenaciously held through faith, bathe the cells of the body with relaxing, healing power.

Now, notice his very next words: "And when ye stand praying, forgive, if ye have ought against any." In other words, get rid of negative emotions of resentment, jealousy, envy, or hatred, or God cannot answer the prayer for health. Of course not! These negative emotions will counterbalance the desire for health and make it impossible for God to give us the desire of our hearts.

All negative emotions result in tension, in a tightening of muscles and fibers. Such constriction cuts off the free flow of blood, causing engorgement of blood or congestion, and consequent inflammation, swelling, and fever. Doctors tell us that as soon as the emotional tension is relieved the blood begins to flow freely and the congestion soon disappears. The power of prayer and quiet affirmations in the presence of God is a spiritual therapy that works wonders in the relief of emotional strain and bodily congestion. As Dr. Richard C. Cabot of the Harvard Medical School used to tell his students, the body is biased in favor of health and the healing power will flow naturally to every cell in the body if we employ spiritual resources.

At this point someone may say that he has always supposed that germs were the cause of most illnesses. Well, they are always present. But listen to Dr. Rebecca Beard on that: "We do not deny that germs enter the picture, but we are confident that the germs are accessories after the fact. Something must happen in the body before the germs have an opportunity to do their work. Germs, like the poor, are always with us. Why do they affect us at one time and not another? *Because the germs can begin their work only when the cell resistance is lowered.* Due to congestion, the food supply as well as the oxygen for the cells is partially cut off, and this lowers the resistance of the cells so the germs find a favorable opening. Infection then is added to congestion. When the tension is released and the congestion is broken up, the cells regain their normal resistance and the germs have no chance." *

The devastating effects of worry were reflected on the faces of the crowds which listened to Jesus. So, he said: "*Do not worry* about life, wondering what you will have to eat or drink, or about your body, wondering what you will have to wear. Is not life more important than food, and the body than clothes? . . . For these are all things the heathen are in pursuit of, and your heavenly Father knows well that you need all this. But you must make his kingdom, and up-

* *Everyman's Search*, p. 29.

rightness before him, your greatest care, and you will have all these other things besides." (Matt. 6:25, 32–33, Goodspeed's translation.)

How modern Jesus was in his insistent warnings against worry and fear and all other negative emotions! Dr. Beard gives us this penetrating analysis of how some people get diabetes. "Early researchers in psychosomatics found something most interesting about diabetes. They discovered that deep grief uses up more energy than any other emotion. In acute grief the body pours quantities of sugar into the blood stream to furnish the energy needed. If the period of grief is not unduly prolonged, the body will adjust itself, but if the grief is submerged and cherished over a long period the body continues to respond in the only way it knows by replenishing the system with more sugar. The point made is that this is a perfectly normal reaction to an emotional stimulus. The abnormal side of the picture is a grief submerged and carried in the heart, or subconscious, so that the body continues to pour blood sugar into the blood stream over months and years until the pancreas cells are exhausted. The pancreas cells make the insulin which causes sugar to burn up into energy, but with this excessive amount of sugar coming in all the time, the pancreas cells simply cannot keep up with it, and they go on a 'sit down strike.' They are too tired to try to keep up with the emotions, and stop making insulin. Then the blood sugar is not burned up and runs free in the blood stream, and we call it sugar diabetes." * Exces-

* *Ibid.* p. 59.

sive fear, or any other negative emotion long indulged, may cause the same disease.

Mothers who nurse their babies are warned these days that a worried or fearful mental attitude affects the milk in such a way as to be harmful to the babe. *Time* magazine pointed this out in comparing the content of the 1914 "Infant Care" with the 1951 edition. This Children's Bureau booklet from the Government Printing Office has had a circulation of twenty-eight million copies since 1914. But what a change there has been in the content! Says *Time*:

"The wisdom of 1914 noted that 'the milk of each animal . . . is especially adapted to the requirements of the young of that species.' This alone was supposed to convince every mother that she must nurse her child. As of 1951: 'It is the spirit in which you feed your baby that counts, rather than the particular kind of milk he gets.' "

Recently, in the Des Moines *Register*, my eye caught a headline, "More Danger in Sleep Pill Than in Dope." The article stated that recent studies of the use of barbiturates (sleeping pills) had led medical authorities to believe that some of these drugs were more of a menace to society than heroin or morphine. The matron who thinks a pink pill as much of a bedtime necessity as brushing her teeth, the tense businessman who gulps a white capsule to ease his nerves before an important business conference, the college student who swallows a yellow "goof ball" to breeze through an examination, and the actor who takes a "blue angel" to bolster his self-confidence are aware that excessive use of barbiturates is "not good for the system" but are ignorant of the extent of the hazard.

Health Commissioner John F. Mahoney of Des Moines recently declared that sleeping pills were causing a steady increase in human wreckage in that city, and that effective control of their sale was no longer possible on a local basis. Interstate traffic in these drugs was so widespread, he said, that new federal laws were necessary to regulate their use.

Herbert Wieder and James M. Toolan, senior psychiatrists at Bellevue Hospital in New York, have said there is no doubt that sleeping pills are habit-forming, very dangerous except under controlled use, destructive of nerve tissue; and sudden withdrawal of them from a user could cause convulsions and psychosis. "Addiction to sleeping pills is far more dangerous to the patient and to society than is heroin addiction," according to Dr. Wieder. "During the period of barbiturate intoxication, the user may be far more aggressive, acting out angers and sex behavior, than a heroin addict."

Dr. Wilbur Miller, head of the Psychopathic Hospital in in Iowa City, stated in a recent address to the local Kiwanis Club on the use of drugs that he had attended a party the night before and had drunk two cups of coffee at one o'clock; after that, he had taken a good dose of sleeping pills to get to sleep, and he was still so drugged in the morning that he had to take a wake-up pill before he could get going. That was all right in an emergency and under a doctor's orders, he explained; but millions of Americans live so fast and burn the candle at both ends so regularly that they are becoming serious drug addicts through the use of sleeping pills. Youths take sleeping pills with beer to get a "high" feeling. The output of sleeping pills in 1949 in this country was 672,000 pounds, or 24 pills for every man, woman, and child. Overdoses of sleeping pills caused more than 1,000 deaths, and the figures had risen sharply every year since 1949!

The cause of this alarming condition is not far to seek. The pace of modern life is ever faster and faster. Deaths on the highways run higher and higher as people drive at terrific speeds. More and more people are drinking greater quantities of liquor in the effort to run away from it all. Ten billion dollars a year is spent for this artificial solvent of men's ills. Our hospitals are overflowing with people, many of whom have lost their way in life.

There is only one sure answer that I know of—the Sermon on the Mount. There we are told to give up worry and fear and hatred and jealousy and envy, indulgence in which is like building a house on sand, a house sure to fall when the floods come; to pass no more judgments upon other people, so that we may not have judgment passed upon us; but to seek earnestly for the kingdom of God and his uprightness—then the things we have worried about will automatically come right. It is little wonder that the following words of the Master have been called the most beautiful and comforting words ever uttered: "Come unto me, all ye that labour and are heavy laden, and I will give you *rest.*"

Three or four years ago, I received a letter from a lady in a sanitarium in Missouri. She was very ill. She had felt sure she was going to die. She was obsessed with fears and worries of all kinds. She was separated from her husband. Her weight had slipped from a normal 180 pounds to 110. She could hardly lift her hand from the bed. Although the doctor had not diagnosed her illness as cancer, she was sure she was about to die of it.

She wrote that she had seen a copy of *Handles of Power*, and that she would like to have the book and the accompanying Silent Communion cards. I sent the book and cards at once. Three months later, another letter from her was a joy to read. She had been using the affirmations continuously to feed her deep or unconscious mind with courage, faith, hope, and love. Here, for example, is the soul food on card number one, "For Building a New Life": "Infinite possibilities for growth and unfoldment lie ahead as I give myself over completely into the hands of God. Through silent communion with Him, new harmony and health and vitality are being manifested in my body, mind and affairs. I can do all things through Him who strengtheneth me." Here is the affirmation on another card: "I am expressing the radiant light and the contagious joy of the kingdom of Heaven throughout this day!" And a third: "I am the temple of God. He is always with me, the life of my life, the light of my seeing; and I am resolved to reflect his poise through his peace that passes understanding." The card on "Shifting the Load" says: "I confess each fear, each worry, each sin to thee. With entire confidence and faith I affirm: The load is gone! I am free!"

She came to understand the relation of the conscious mind to the unconscious, to grasp the meaning of Jesus's "single eye" philosophy of life, of the fact that every fearful, negative thought adversely affects the entire body, while every loving, faith-filled thought sends a stream of healing power to the last cell. The nurse who had attended Mrs. M. in her illness told me about the momentous day when she decided to quit using the sleeping pills that were destroying her nerve tissue and about her steadfast use of the cards day and night to keep tuned to infinite resources.

Her improvement in physical well-being was directly proportional to the revolutionary change in her mental and spiritual outlook. Soon she was up and around, gaining weight. Came then a letter one day asking my advice about the best way to accomplish a reconciliation with her husband. I referred her to several of the cards that contained powerful affirmations bearing directly on that problem: "As an imitator of God, through the single eye of faith, I am constantly looking for Light, Beauty and Truth in all the relationships of life. . . . I confidently affirm that every difficulty in the field of human relations finds a harmonious solution as I imitate God and walk in humility and love." She finally approached the interview in the spirit of humility, love, and complete confidence, and a beautiful reconciliation resulted.

Having regained her health, she wanted above everything else to help other stricken souls find the way back to joyful living. So, she took a course in nursing and went to work in a hospital where she told others the good news of Christ's healing power.

Silent Communion for Health from Within

Jesus said: "I have spoken all this to you in order that in me you may have peace. In the world you have affliction. But keep up your courage. I have won the victory over the world." (John 16:33, Weymouth translation.)

Forgiveness! Generosity! Understanding! Love! Peace! Radiance! Health from within is mine as I continuously open my mind and body to the creative, dynamic, and celestial inflow of these power-filled words!

CHAPTER SIX

A Quiet Mind—and Health

Some years ago, a friend left a responsible position in Iowa City to work for a large company in a great city. Recently, I heard that he had returned as a patient in our University Hospital. He had come back to put himself under the care of physicians with whom he was personally acquainted. I journeyed to see him.

"They are putting me through a series of tests," he told me, "but so far they have found nothing but hypertension." Hypertension! What a familiar word that has become! "I begin to think I was quite a fool ever to leave this quiet town," he continued. "But I always had a secret ambition to get into the big-time stuff—large responsibilities, a big salary. Well, I made it; an income several times what I got here, fine home, even a yacht—but what good is it without health to enjoy it? I feel so tense and worried and jittery all of the time that I could jump right through my skin." Even as he talked, he squirmed and fidgeted on his bed, trying to relax. "The doctor told me today to quit my present position and get into something else or I'll be a dead duck inside of a year. I can take it or leave it, but that's his final word!"

At a meeting of the American College of Physicians Dr. Edward Weiss of Philadelphia read a paper on diseases of the heart. He cited John Wesley, who wrote in his Journal in 1759 of a woman who had a continuous pain in her abdomen that failed to respond to medical treatment. Wesley found that the pain resulted from the "woman's fretting over the death of her son," and that when she was comforted by religion the pain disappeared. "Why then," asked Wesley, "do not all physicians consider how bodily disorders are caused or influenced by the mind?"

That is precisely what doctors are doing today. Dr. Wilson G. Smillie, professor of public health and preventive medicine at Cornell University Medical College, New York City, recently told the American College of Surgeons that the new diseases are degenerative, those of aging, and affect hearts and arteries; there is no known remedy for them, "and there is not likely to be any until doctors begin preventive measures that involve man's social and economic condition as a probable starting place for these diseases." In other words, the worry and fear indulged by persons who are confused and bewildered by insecurity in the rapidly changing world bring about degeneration of their vital organs.

During the war, certain fliers became convinced that they would be nauseated and sick at high altitudes. Flight surgeons believed that much of this sickness was mentally induced by the fear of it. So they developed a flight chamber in which all the conditions of flying could be simulated.

When Lieutenant H. P. complained of such sickness, they put him in a plane in the pressure chamber. When they told him the pressure was adjusted to that at 17,000 feet (actually, it was equal to that of only 3,000 feet) he became ill; when they told him he was down to 3,000 feet (actually, the pressure was that of 17,000 feet) he felt normal again. He had a psychoneurosis, and was sent to a hospital for rest and "mental treatment."

For admission to the ever growing class of mind-made diseases, the famed neurologist Stanley Cobb of Harvard Medical School recently proposed arthritis. Although the main cause is "an X factor, as yet unknown," Dr. Cobb and his associates reported in the *Journal* of the American Medical Association that "poverty, grief, and family worry" are closely connected with the swollen knuckles and aching joints of rheumatoid arthritis.

In the Massachusetts General Hospital, fifty arthritis patients were interviewed by a psychiatrist or social worker, who asked them to talk freely of their early lives, family relations, work, marriages, and children. Dr. Cobb reported that in all but seven cases there seemed to be a definite relation between their troubles and their arthritis. In twenty-one cases worries and arthritis began about the same time.

A shy, proud little man, known professionally as Tom, has one of the strangest stomachs in existence, described by Stewart Wolf and Harold G. Wolff of New York Hospital in the book *Human Gastric Function.* When Tom was nine years old he drank some hot soup that burned and finally closed his esophagus. For more than forty years he has fed himself through an opening surgeons made in his abdominal wall. This has enabled doctors to peer directly into his stomach and watch carefully what happens to the human stomach under varying conditions. The book is a minute record of the stomach's color, secretion, and activity when Tom felt relaxed and secure as well as when he was full, hungry, worried, or angry.

When an officious office secretary angered Tom his face got red, and so did his stomach. Anger, worry, or fear caused a greatly increased flow of acid secretion whether there was food in the stomach or not. Stomach ulcers are caused by this excess acid, and the doctors conclude that these sick stomachs are best treated through the proper "management of the personality disorder."

Many highway accidents can be traced directly to upset emotions. Anger, grief, fear, and even joy can be dangerous companions in the driver's seat. Dr. Herbert J. Stack, director of the New York University Center for Safety Education, believes that most unsafe driving results from this very cause.

Indeed, who among the readers of these words has not had either an accident or at least a narrow escape from one because the mind was centered, not upon the road, but upon some problem that stirred the emotions?

Mrs. J., an unusually careful driver who had never had an accident, drove into town one morning to consult her attorney about a divorce. When she left his office she was crying and extremely upset. On her way home she had to cross a railroad track. She had driven that way hundreds of times, she knew the train schedule, the tracks were in clear view, the engineer gave his warning whistle; yet Mrs. J. drove directly in front of the express. At the last moment she was seen to make a frenzied effort to escape; but the locomotive killed her instantly. Grief is a dangerous riding companion.

The papers recently reported the accident of Mr. L. After quarreling with his wife at the breakfast table he banged the front door behind him. He slammed the car door as he climbed in, and drove out of the yard at high speed, smack into the side of a passing truck. The damage to the car was $450, and Mr. L. spent several weeks in the hospital. Emotions can be deadly!

A quiet mind and emotional maturity constitute man's most prized possession. Two world wars within a generation have done much to destroy millions of people from within. The dislocations of modern life have taken away from many of us the basic sense of security. Set alongside this loss immature and infantile conceptions of God instilled in many of us in childhood that could not sustain us in the hour of crisis, and we have the fundamental reason for most of our trouble. That is why Liebman's splendid book, *Peace of Mind*, leaped into first place as a best seller.

Peace of mind is possible in spite of anything that this world may do to us. Emotional maturity can become ours—but at a price. It will not come as a result of a new resolution quickly forgotten. A lifetime of crooked, negative thinking cannot be changed overnight. When Paul wrote to his followers in Rome, "Be ye transformed by the renewing of your mind" (Romans 12:2), he described very simply a process whereby a quiet mind can be gradually achieved by any normal person who wants this priceless possession badly enough to concentrate on it over a period of time.

Paul's advice to the Philippians is equally sound: "Whatsoever things are true, whatsoever thing are honest, whatsoever things are just, whatsoever things are pure, whatsoever things are lovely, whatsoever things are of good report . . . think on *these* things. . . . And the peace of God, which passeth all understanding, shall keep your hearts and minds through Christ Jesus." (Philippians 4:8, 7.)

Let us state the same directive in other language: "Concentrate your mind *exclusively* on the truth, honesty, justice, purity, and beauty of God as these attributes of his character find expression in the world, and a peace of mind greater than anything you have ever known or imagined shall be yours even as it was Christ's."

The mind is creative. Every thought creates. Let us not think for one moment that we can achieve the desired results if we dwell upon the worries, fears, and troubles of life for a great portion of our waking days. "If thine eye be *single*," said Jesus, "thy whole body shall be full of light." Single to truth, beauty, and goodness. This does not mean that we are to turn our back on difficulties. It means that we are to face them constructively and positively in the presence of God and with every hope and assurance of finding a solution in the spirit of faith and of love.

Here is a case in point. Mrs. H. had some growing children that did not conform to the adult pattern of perfection which she had foolishly set for them. She mistook their growing pains for heinous sins. She was filled with anxiety and panic as she sought to compel them to be "good" according to her rather restrictive and puritanical patterns. She was bearing still another child which she was sure would also turn out to be "a little devil."

Full of panic and fear, she took to her bed and stayed there five months. Then when she was listening to a religious service on the radio she heard these words: "Fear thou not; for I am with thee: be not dismayed; for I am thy God: I will strengthen thee; yea, I will help thee; yea, I will uphold thee with the right hand of my righteousness." (Isaiah 41:10.)

A neighbor, who had come into a great faith of her own by the very technique here set down, was sitting by her bed. When Mrs. H. wistfully said that she would give anything to be able to prove the truth of Isaiah's great words of assurance, the neighbor replied: "But you can. Let us write that verse down on a card. Keep that card under your pillow, and slowly and meaningfully repeat it many times a day until it comes alive and sinks deep into your heart."

She did it. Day after day she kept repeating the thrilling affirmation over and over until she became aware that God was present, that he was alive in her heart. It was some time later that the neighbor saw her again, and then she was a different woman. She was up and around the house, doing her own work with a smile on her face and a song on her lips. "I have found the secret," she said. "I know God. The fear is gone. And my children have changed."

Norman Vincent Peale, minister of the Marble Collegiate Church in New York City, once made a valuable suggestion: that two collections might well be taken in every church every Sunday morning. The second would not be of money. Instead, the members of the congregation would be asked to write out their worries, fear and guilt complexes on a card. They would not need to sign their names, because God would recognize them anyway. The ushers would then pass the plates and the minister would receive them, take them to the altar, and solemnly give the people's troubles and sins to God.

To this new and practical and psychologically sound form of confessional, I would add one suggestion: Let the ushers pass out Silent Communion cards as the people leave. Nature hates a vacuum. The anxieties, fears, and sins that occupy the citadel of consciousness must be replaced by love and truth and hope, or the old sins will take unto themselves others, and the last state will be worse than the first, even as Jesus said.

The cards would contain such powerful affirmations as Romans 8:35, 37–38, directions to repeat *again and again* until the deep mind has been filled and renewed with God's own strength: "Who shall separate us from the love of Christ? Shall tribulation, or distress, or persecution, or famine, or nakedness, or peril, or sword? . . . No, in all these things we are more than conquerors through him who loved us. For I am sure that neither death, nor life, nor angels, nor principalities, nor things present, nor things to come, nor powers, nor height, nor depth, nor anything else in all creation, will be able to separate us from the love of God in Christ Jesus our Lord." (Revised Standard Version.)

Look through your New Testament, and you will notice that the words of both Paul and Jesus contain an abundance of short, pointed, powerful affirmations. They both used them for the unfoldment of their own lives. Luke says that Jesus *grew* in wisdom, in stature, and in favor with God and man. This is the method that he used, and he promised us that if we would follow him we should do even greater things. But the tragic barrier to the fulfillment of his glorious expectations for us has been our negative, doubt-filled, vacillating thoughts; full of faith today, full of doubt, cynicism, and despair tomorrow. The chapters that follow will contain the true life stories of people who have accomplished seeming miracles by stepping confidently and boldly out upon the positive, faith-dominated promises of God. Do you sincerely want greater health and wholeness of body, mind, and affairs? Very well. You have but to use this technique faithfully over a period of time, and this tremendous boon shall be yours. Power to you, my friend!

I have a treasure which I prize
The like I cannot find;
There's nothing like it in the earth—
It is a quiet mind.

But 'tis not that I'm stupefied,
Or senseless, dull, or blind;

'Tis God's own peace within my soul
Which forms my quiet mind.

And what may be tomorrow's cross
I never seek to find;
The God mind says: Leave that to me,
And keep a quiet mind.

The love of God within my heart,
My heart to His doth bind;
This is the mind of heaven on earth,
This is my quiet mind.
—*Author unknown*

Silent Communion for the Development of a Quiet Mind

I believe in the Power of the Living God; a Power that is within me; the gift of the God who made me in His own glorious image. "My peace I give unto you," said Jesus, so, "Let not your heart be troubled, neither let it be afraid." This is the mind of heaven on earth; this is my quiet mind.

CHAPTER SEVEN

Three Levels of Consciousness

Psychologists usually talk about two levels of consciousness. The conscious or waking mind is thought to represent roughly about a tenth of the mind. That part of us can think and reason and arrive at certain judgments after sifting the wheat from the chaff. This critical faculty decides what is true or false according to the light we have at the moment. The unconscious, or nine-tenths of the mind, is uncritical. Its main business seems to be to register what the conscious mind dwells upon and to bring *that* into manifestation. Thus, if the general tenor of the conscious mind is characterized by faith, hope, and love, the deep mind must bring that into manifestation; and if one's dominant thought is characterized by fear, doubt, hatred, and insecurity, that too will be reflected in one's life.

Realizing these truths, Jesus was always talking about the necessity of positive thinking and faith. In the ninth chapter of Mark, for example, we have the story of the father of an epileptic son being brought to Jesus's disciples for healing, but they could do nothing for him. So, the father brought the lad to Jesus, who healed him. To the father, he said: "*If thou canst believe, all things are possible to him that believeth.*" To the crestfallen disciples he explained that difficult cases of this kind responded only to fasting and prayer. Fasting enables one to concentrate with a clearer mind. Thus, when the mind is held at the focal point of the desire, with unwavering faith, the healing power of God is released. Results come to anyone who believes consistently without letting fear and doubt take over. God plays no favorites: "All things are possible to him that believeth."

We have said that the unconscious is uncritical, and that it takes at face value what it receives from the conscious; if the person is under hypnosis, with the conscious mind asleep, the unconscious will receive uncritically a suggestion from the hypnotist and proceed to carry out the suggestion after the subject awakens.

The second chapter of *Something to Stand On* describes an experiment with Don Hout, one of the student leaders at the University of Iowa. While Don was under hypnosis a graduate student in psychology told him that the letter *e* had been taken from his alphabet, and that he would not be able to spell any word correctly that had *e* in it until nine o'clock the next morning; that he would not know that he had ever seen the letter *e* in his life. After Don returned to consciousness a number of us worked on him to try to get him to recognize the letter *e*, but to no avail. The next morning in an eight-thirty class, he took notes but left out all the *e*'s. It was not until nine o'clock that he suddenly realized what he had done.

That is why, dear friends, it is so imperative for us to keep our God-given critical mind ever alert to sift the true from the false in the realm of religion as well as in all other fields. Autosuggestion is merely the act of saying to ourselves that we believe this or that, after critical examination. Faith is but the acceptance of a positive suggestion. Doubt is the rejection of a suggestion. So, let us not be afraid of the word "autosuggestion" or assume, as many do, that autosuggestion is "believing something that isn't so," or that there is no objective validity connected with it.

As David Seabury says: "Faith is, of course, as closely related to autosuggestion as it is to prayer. *Belief is an autosuggestion*, or better put, *an autosuggestion when accepted becomes a belief*. Of this we have an example in the healing technique at the shrine of Lourdes. The 'miracles' that take place there are in every sense typical of those performed by Jesus. The hours of intense worship are not unlike those of a trance. The extreme subjectivity induces an utter concentration on the nature of the health desired. It is vividly and repetitively pictured as the prayer takes place. To say that the cures which result are autosuggestion is merely to reaffirm the power of faith." * It is the law of mind and spirit at work after the manner that a wise and loving God has made us. Any thoughtful doctor will admit that thousands of people die when they might get well because they *think* their time has come. This shows the power of negative suggestion. Others live when even the doctor has given them up, because they are determined to live and because they

* Seabury, *How Jesus Heals Our Minds Today* (Boston: Little, Brown & Co., 1940), pp. 265–266.

say so positively again and again. *This shows the unbelievable power of positive suggestion.*

When the disciples had failed to heal the epileptic boy, and they asked Jesus why, he said: "Because of your unbelief: for verily I say unto you, If ye have faith as a grain of mustard seed, ye shall say unto this mountain, Remove hence yonder place; and it shall remove; and nothing shall be impossible unto you" (Matt. 17:20). A grain of mustard seed is the smallest kind of seed, but when it is planted and left alone in good ground it grows into a tree. It has within it, therefore, infinite possibilities for accomplishing great things. So it is with men who have faith in God. Thus does God work through these two levels of consciousness.

But there is still a third level. Somewhere in the deep mind is a meeting place where the Infinite and Creative Mind of God makes contact with our finite human minds and discloses truth and beauty not known to us before. That contact is the source of what we call *inspiration* in art, music, literature, science, philosophy, and religion. It may come when we are relaxed and listening to what the Universal Mind has to give us; or it may flash us an unexpected message when we are doing something totally unrelated to the lovely thing that suddenly impinges on the field of consciousness.

Mozart got the idea for the *Magic Flute* quintet while playing billiards. He tells us that while "taking a drive or walking after a good meal, or in the night when I cannot sleep, thoughts crowd into my mind as easily as you could wish." Handel, after a period of despair and total unproductiveness, suddenly heard music that was not of earth. For three days and nights he sat motionless gazing into space "in heaven" without being conscious of even the food the houseboy placed before him. Then he rapturously seized pen and paper and gave the world the *Messiah* with its thrilling and matchless Hallelujah Chorus that will inspire the souls of men forever. The prolific Haydn, with 104 symphonies and hundreds of other compositions to his credit, wrote that when his work did not advance he would retire to a quiet place for prayer, and "immediately ideas come to me."

The great Blake declared: "I have written the poem . . . without premeditation and even against my will." Van Gogh once told friends that at times he experienced "a terrible lucidity," when nature appeared glorious and he was hardly conscious of himself as pictures came to him in a kind of dream demanding expression on canvas. Sir Isaac Newton, like most intuitive mathematicians, usually got a result before he could prove it; indeed one great discovery of his on the roots of equations was not proved until two hundred years later.

George Washington Carver, the slave boy who was once traded for a race horse, astonished the scientific world with his intuitive methods, benefiting the rural South more than any other American has ever done. After studying agriculture in Ames, Iowa, he hastened south to Tuskegee Institute to help rescue his people from the blight and poverty resulting from their ruined land. He told them to substitute sweet potatoes and peanuts for cotton and then he proceeded to astound the world by developing from the sweet potato and the peanut more than three hundred separate products. Not only was the land thereby enriched and restored to fertility, but these many products were processed and sold, raising the standard of life in the South enormously.

Called to Washington to testify before a Congressional committee on the problem of southern agriculture, he was told he could have but ten minutes at the end of a hard, grueling day. At the end of one hour, when he tried to cut short his testimony, the committee—including John Nance Garner and Alben Barkley—insisted that he go on. The three hundred products he had found in the lowly peanut were too much for them!

"No books ever go into my laboratory," he said to an audience in Marble Collegiate Church in New York City. "The thing that I am to do and the way of doing it come to me. I never have to grope for methods; the method is revealed at the moment I am inspired to create something new. Without God to draw aside the curtain, I would be helpless." On another occasion he said: "My prayers seem to be more an attitude than anything else. I indulge in very little lip service, but ask the Great Creator silently, daily, and often many times a day, to permit me to speak to Him through the three great Kingdoms of the world which He has created—the animal, mineral and vegetable Kingdoms—

to understand their relations to each other, and our relations to them and to the great God Who made all of us. I ask Him daily and often momently to give me wisdom, understanding and bodily strength to do His will; hence I am asking and receiving all the time." *

When I heard this gentle old colored man speak to a huge audience in Minneapolis some years ago, I knew that there was a level of consciousness somewhere in his deep mind where God revealed to him secrets never before known to mankind.

Let us offer a word of caution at this point. Receiving inspiration from the Universal Mind is no lazy man's royal road to knowledge. The recipient of such knowledge must do his part. George Washington Carver spent years of arduous preparation mastering agriculture before he received any secrets from God. Dickens had slaved to become a master story-teller before the complete plot for *A Christmas Carol* flashed through his mind while he was walking along a street in Manchester one night before Christmas in 1843. Although he was working on *Martin Chuzzlewit* at the time and his publishers were waiting for copy, the tight, wicked old Scrooge and his magic trips into the past with a ghost would give him no rest until he had given the world the greatest Christmas story of all time. The same was true of Harriet Beecher Stowe as she wrote *Uncle Tom's Cabin.* "The Lord wrote it," she declared. The scene in which

* Rackham Holt, *George Washington Carver: An American Biography* (New York: Doubleday & Co., 1943), pp. 265, 295–296.

Uncle Tom was flogged came to her in a vision during a communion service. As though in a trance she walked home fighting to keep the tears back. She went straight to her desk and wrote out the vision as she had seen it before the altar. When she read it to her children, they wept convulsively. So did millions of others around the world. The doom of slavery was sealed when *Uncle Tom's Cabin* was finished.

On a night in October, 1920, the young Canadian doctor Frederick Grant Banting was working over his next day's lecture. The subject was diabetes. He had read everything he could lay his hands on, but his brain was weary over the conflicting theories as to how it might be treated. Finally, he laid his books aside and went to bed. At two o'clock in the morning he awakened, switched on his light, and wrote three sentences in his notebook: "Tie off pancreatic duct of dogs. Wait six to eight weeks for degeneration. Remove residue and extract." Then he turned his light off and went back to sleep. Those three magic sentences led to the discovery of insulin which controls diabetes, a problem that had baffled the whole medical fraternity up to that time. Banting's hard work had prepared him for the tip that came from the Universal Mind.

Of a somewhat different character was the inspiration from beyond the veil that came to Joan of Arc in the fifteenth century. I rode into the tiny village of Domremy, France, one Sunday morning toward the close of World War I. It was church time, and I parked my car and entered the little Catholic church where she used to worship.

After hearing the mass, I went to her home and thence out to sit on the rural hillside where she watched her sheep.

In that peaceful setting I recalled her thrilling story: France is on the brittle edge of the abyss of destruction. The Church is distracted by the Great Schism, with three rival Popes pitted against one another. Three competing armies are in the field. The King of England commands in the west, the Duke of Burgundy in the north, and the weak Dauphin maintains a precarious authority south of the Loire. The helpless French peasants suffer pillaging and plundering everywhere. The situation for France appears utterly hopeless.

Under these circumstances an illiterate peasant girl of seventeen begins hearing voices which instruct her to save her country by making a perilous journey to Chinon, through three hundred miles of rough country infested by marauding gangs. There she must tell the Dauphin of her mission to lead an army, to raise the siege of Orléans, and then to conduct the King to Rheims for coronation.

For two days she waits to be admitted to the royal presence in Chinon. The greedy, drunken courtiers cannot believe that a simple, ignorant peasant girl can possibly do anything for a France that is on the verge of ruin. They finally decide to test her. Dressing the Dauphin just like all the others at the court, they tell her to use her divine guidance in picking him out of the crowd. This she does instantly, though she has had no idea what he looked like. Point by point she wins her way in spite of all of the opposition. When the King offers her a sword she refuses it, saying her voices have instructed her to carry a certain sword that would be found hidden behind the altar in the Church of St. Catherine of Fierbois. To everyone's astonishment, they find the sword there!

The rest of the story is well known. Joan did raise the siege of Orléans and save France, and she did conduct the Dauphin to Rheims for coronation. Then, like her Master, she was betrayed, sold for a few pieces of silver, and burned at the stake, while her King made not a single effort to save her. Like her Master, she did more to redeem France from degeneracy by her martyr's death than she could have accomplished by living to a ripe old age. In the heaven to which she went, she was far better off than the miserable wretches who sent her there.

You and I may not receive any secrets from the Universal Mind comparable to a Carver, a Banting, a Mozart, a Dickens, or a Joan of Arc, but God will speak to us if we carefully prepare ourselves and listen regularly to the still, small voice deep within.

Silent Communion for Listening to the Voice of the Eternal

Speak to Him thou for He hears, and Spirit with Spirit can meet—
Closer is He than breathing, and nearer than hands and feet.

—Tennyson

"Be still, and know that I am God" (Psalm 46:10).

My heart is the home of God, who is the Spirit of Love and Truth. I am listening, relaxed and quiet and confident, for God's Spirit of Truth to guide me in whatsoever I do and say. Herein lies my True Peace.

CHAPTER EIGHT

The Conquest of Futility

A sense of overwhelming futility once flooded the mind and soul of Elijah. Queen Jezebel, tired of his righteous crusades, sent a messenger to tell the great prophet that she would end his life within twenty-four hours. The terror-stricken soul took to his heels and ran a day's journey into the wilderness and sat down under a juniper tree and begged God, "Take away my life."

He was very tired, as people usually are when mired in pessimism, and so he lay down and had a good sleep. Then he fled another forty days and hid in a cave. There the word of the Lord came to him, asking what he was doing there. He told the Lord how wicked everybody was and concluded, "I, even I only, am left" true to Jehovah, "and they seek my life, to take it away."

He was then ordered to "stand upon the mount before the Lord." A strong wind broke up some of the rocks, "but the Lord was not in the wind." Came then an earthquake and a fire, but the Lord was not in them. This violence was followed by "a still small voice"—the voice of God—which ordered *action.* He was to go forthwith to Damascus and anoint Hazael to be king over Syria and Jehu to be king over Israel. After all, said the Lord, "I have left me seven thousand in Israel, all the knees which have not bowed unto Baal." With these new kings, life would go on and the battle would be won. But faint-hearted Elijah's usefulness was over, and so his final act was to be the bestowal of his mantle upon Elisha, the new prophet.

There are many Elijahs in the world today, overwhelmed by a sense of utter futility. They point to Korea or French Indo-China or Egypt or Russia and say the foreign situation is an insoluble mess. They point to graft and scandal and high taxes and the national debt in our own land and say we are lost. The situation *is* bad. But was there ever a time when it wasn't?

Do you sigh for the good old days? Even stout-hearted old Benjamin Franklin took pen in hand one day and wrote: "Some indeed among us are not so much grieved for the present state of our affairs, as apprehensive of the future. They observe that no Revenue is sufficient without Economy, and that the most plentiful Income of a whole People from the natural Productions of their Country may be dissipated in vain and needless Expenses, and Poverty be introduced in the place of Affluence."

Well, if history offers one great lesson for our futility-ridden days, it is that man's greatest achievements have almost always come in years of darkness, and they have stemmed from individuals who were fully cognizant of the peril but kept their minds focused on an unconquerable God of Power and Righteousness who could never be defeated. Jesus was a member of a conquered people whose taxes were exorbitant and who suffered such indignities daily at the hands of the hated Romans that they were always on the point of armed but hopeless rebellion. Yet, out of that time came the Sermon on the Mount!

Writes Dr. James T. Fisher, noted psychiatrist: "If you were to take the sum total of all the authoritative articles ever written by the most qualified of psychologists and psychiatrists on the subject of mental hygiene, if you were to combine them and refine them and cleave out the excess verbiage, if you were to take the whole of the meat and none of the parsley, and if you were to have these unadulterated bits of pure scientific knowledge concisely expressed by the most capable of living poets, you would have an awkward and incomplete summation of the Sermon on the Mount." * Yet, that series of faith-filled pronouncements came during one of the darkest and most hopeless periods in the history of mankind.

After Jesus died on a cross, there began the march of eleven men across the centuries, common ordinary men who caught his matchless spirit and faith and added others to their number until they conquered the Roman Empire. Their stories, built around the words of their Master, were written in Greek to form the twenty-seven books of our New Testament.

Early in the fifth century after Christ, St. Jerome made his way to the very cave where Jesus had been born in

* James T. Fisher and Lowell S. Hawley, *A Few Buttons Missing* (Philadelphia: J. B. Lippincott Co., 1951).

Bethlehem and translated those books from the Greek into the Latin so that the peoples of Europe could read the words of life. While he worked, he heard that the Eternal City, symbol of the permanence of Christendom, had been sacked by the Goths. "What is left if Rome perishes?" he wrote. *But he kept right on working just the same.* There followed the seven hundred years of blight known as the Dark Ages, but Jerome's great Latin Vulgate translation became the basis for the flowering of the Renaissance. In the sweep of the centuries the work of St. Jerome, man of faith, created far more than Alaric the Goth destroyed.

Through all history there runs a stream of dauntless, high faith, and courage in the face of terrific odds—a resilience of spirit and a stubborn denial that human life can be defeated. I never take a canoe trip along the Canadian border but the trees remind me of the fact that the whole universe has a growing edge that cannot and will not be denied. That north country is a mass of volcanic rock. But look at any shore line and you will see beautiful pine trees by the tens of thousands growing out of tiny cracks in the rocks, exultantly tossing their pine-scented arms toward the sky. What magnificent effrontery! They represent a *life principle*, that of ongoing and growth; and so they go ahead and *do* what common sense and prudence would say cannot be done.

The men in the vanguard of the human race have deep within them the same dauntless courage and quiet faith. Abraham Lincoln came to the Presidency in 1861 when, in his own phrase, "the heavens were hung with black." The country he loved was divided and torn by the seemingly unsolvable problem of slavery. Certainly his own record up to that time would not seem to indicate that he should be entertaining any illusions about how successful a leader he would be. Here is that record:

Failed in business, 1831; defeated for Illinois Legislature, '32; again failed in business, '33; elected to Legislature, '34; sweetheart died, '35; had nervous breakdown, '36; defeated for Speaker of Illinois House, '38; defeated for Presidential Elector, '40; defeated for Congress, '43; elected to Congress, '46; defeated for Congress, '48; defeated for United States Senate, '55; defeated for Vice President, '56; defeated for Senate, '58; elected President, '60.

Yet, nearly a century later, Lincoln is seen to be the greatest President the United States has ever had. The very hopelessness of the hour called forth that ever resurgent something which God Almighty has always given to humble, seeking souls in their hour of anguish and trial. That fact ought to banish our enervating sense of futility today.

Before sitting down to write this evening, I picked up my Bible and read the parable of the tares: "Another parable put he forth unto them, saying, The kingdom of heaven is likened unto a man which sowed good seed in his field: But while men slept, his enemy came and sowed tares among the wheat, and went his way. But when the blade was sprung up, and brought forth fruit, then appeared the tares also. So the servants of the householder came and said unto him, Sir, didst not thou sow good seed in thy field? from whence then hath it tares? He said unto them, An enemy hath done this. The servants said unto him, Wilt thou then that we go and gather them up? But he said, Nay; lest while ye gather up the tares, ye root up also the wheat with them. Let both grow together until the harvest: and in the time of harvest I will say to the reapers, Gather ye together first the tares, and bind them in bundles to burn them: but gather the wheat into my barn." (Matt. 13:24–30.)

Our sense of futility comes from seeing so many tares growing with the wheat. Some ministers spend most of Sunday morning denouncing war, alcohol, infidelity, gambling, grafting, and many other such evils. These blotches on the face of our society need to be denounced now and then, but I must confess that, the older I grow, the more I feel the need of bringing the *positive* approach to bear on all our many problems. As Jesus said, we may easily so concentrate on the tares that we root out the wheat and have nothing left to harvest.

How well Jesus knew the human heart! We can focus our minds so steadily upon the evils we are fighting that we lose all sense of the beauty of the kingdom of goodness we are defending. Elijah knocked himself clear out of the fight by doing just that. He fought the false prophets of Baal so hard that he was overcome by futility and ended up under a juniper tree whining, "I, even I only, am left." God told him that he was wrong by as much as seven thousand, and that what he needed was a *positive* approach: "*Go*, and anoint two kings to carry on the business of living. Then give your mantle to another and get out of the way!" Elijah was ruined by overconcentrating on tares.

It is significant that the parable of the tares is immediately followed by the parable of the grain of mustard seed: "Another parable put he forth unto them, saying, The kingdom of heaven is like to a grain of mustard seed, which a man took, and sowed in his field: which indeed is the least of all seeds: but when it is grown, it is the greatest among herbs, and becometh a tree, so that the birds of the air come and lodge in the branches thereof." (Matt. 13:31–32.)

What is the most attractive and powerful force against evil in any community in the long run? It is a radiant, humble, unpretentious, love-dominated soul who goes quietly about his business. All unconsciously he makes others long for the precious thing that emanates from his God-conscious soul. His is the power of the grain of mustard seed.

America's greatest danger today is that she tends to fight the tares of Communism so intently that she endangers the very freedoms she seeks to protect; that she may spend so large a proportion of her wealth for weapons of war that she will have nothing left for the Point Four program of positive action in helping the downtrodden, poverty-stricken millions in other countries to find a higher standard of life—the only constructive way to end the threat of Communism.

A true story will illustrate what we have been trying to say: When Sherman Rogers was twenty years of age, the foreman of the Idaho logging camp where he was working went to town one winter day, leaving him in charge of the men with instructions to act like the real boss and fire any man who refused to take orders.

To Rogers that was a God-given opportunity to fire

Tony, a glum, sour-looking Italian whose job it was to keep Hill Number Two sanded so that the giant sleds would not run over the horses. As he approached he saw Tony heating a shovelful of sand over a small fire. The mercury was at zero, and Tony was evidently cold; but instead of warming his body by the fire he was warming sand!

At that moment the owner of the camp noticed Rogers watching and said: "Don't bother Tony, if that is what you have in mind as the temporary foreman. I've been logging forty years, and Tony is the most reliable man I ever had. He's a grouch and hates everybody; but the fact remains that he is on the job before anybody else, and he never quits until everyone else has gone. There hasn't been an accident on Hill Two in the eight years Tony has been sander, although men and horses were killed every year before that."

Rogers says that, instead of firing the man, he said: "Good morning, Tony. I'm the boss today, and I had every intention of firing you until the owner of this camp told me what a good man you were." And he repeated the owner's remarks, word for word. "Why he no tell me dat eight year 'go?" asked Tony as he dropped the shovelful of sand he was heating. And the tears started running down his cheeks.

That night, when the teamsters came in to wash up, Tony was the one topic of conversation. "That guy has thrown enough sand today to sand a dozen hills," said one. "He's flown up and down as though he had wings, and he has actually smiled all day."

Tony dragged Rogers to his tiny log home for dinner to

meet Marie, the mother of his four "keeds," and told her in Italian what had happened that morning. She ran around the table, threw her arms around the kind American's neck, and kissed him. "Marie feel like Christmas when I tell her," said Tony.

That night Marie told the visitor how difficult it was for the children in school because of the contemptuous remarks of other children about the poor clothes of the little "wops" and their funny looks; and when he saw her put them to bed, heard her pray God in broken English to help them grow up good Americans and please try to make American children understand her children and stop calling them "wops," he decided on a course of action.

The next day Rogers went to the school, had the four Italians excused for half an hour while he pleaded with the other children to give them a chance by treating them as kindly and helpfully as they would hope to be treated if they were in Italy. That was the beginning of happier days for Tony's "keeds."

Rogers did not see Tony again for twelve years. Then the big Italian had become the successful superintendent of railroad construction in one of the biggest logging outfits in the West. Said the beaming Tony: "If it no be for da one minute you talka to me back in Idaho, I keel somebody some day. One minute she change my whole life. You spent half-hour down in schoolroom—and she change lives my keeds too." Then he added: "I wonder why more people don't try understand more and hate less."

Why indeed! Action and still more action of the faith,

hope, love variety would sweeten our sour souls and dissipate the fog of futility that engulfs us. Live with the following declaration a few days, and see what happens to you. One thing we promise—whatever happens will be good. You will like it; and so will your friends!

Silent Communion for the Conquest of My Sense of Futility

The writer of the Twenty-third Psalm in the long ago knew how to conquer his sense of futility and to draw courage from the vast storehouse of the Infinite. My resources are the same as his.

The Lord is my Shepherd—now.
He leadeth me beside the still waters—at this very moment.
He restoreth my soul—constantly.
Yea, though I walk through the valley of the shadow of death, thou art with me—always.
What else really matters?

CHAPTER NINE

The Eight-Notched Key

The Sermon on the Mount contains more spiritual insight and clear directives for happy, healthy, successful living than have ever before or since been packed into so few words. The discourse opens with the eight Beatitudes, describing an *inwardness of spirit* without which no man can enter the kingdom of heaven. People have seldom understood them because of the way they are phrased in the King James Version. For this reason, millions of good people have failed to use this *eight-notched Spiritual Key* to the abundant life.

Moses laid out an intricate system of laws, ordinances, and taboos that had to be *outwardly* observed in minute detail if God's wrath were to be avoided. They were couched almost exclusively in the negative. Although their observance is absolutely essential, eight of the ten commandments are in negative terms. You must *not* commit adultery, or steal, or kill, or bear false witness. Where you find a positive commandment like, "Remember the Sabbath day to keep it holy," you also find the priests hedging it about with a whole series of negations: don't travel, don't cook, don't do any housework, don't work in the field. The rabbis then took each of these and restricted the people still further: don't comb your hair on the Sabbath lest you pull out one hair and thus find yourself guilty of "reaping." If you wish to visit a distant friend on the Sabbath, take an old pair of shoes over there earlier in the week. Where your old shoes are is "home," and therefore you will just be going from one room of your home to another! There were more than six hundred such rules of conduct for the religious man to follow, and if he broke one of them he was guilty of violating them all.

With this arid externalism Jesus found himself in deep conflict. He dealt only with general principles that had to do with *mental states*, for he knew that if one's mental attitude was sound all else would come right. He was concerned only with the *inwardness* of an act, and not with its external observance. For him, internalism must replace externalism if the spirit is to be in tune with God: "*God is a Spirit: and they that worship him must worship him in spirit and in truth.*" When the Pharisees accused him of breaking the Sabbath by healing a man that day, and when they accused his disciples of reaping on the Sabbath because they picked and ate wheat while passing through a field, he said: "The sabbath was made for man, not man for the sabbath." In both cases he looked at the *motive* and found it good. Thus, out went the whole abominable externalism of Sabbath observance which had made the day a nightmare instead of a worshipful experience.

The Beatitudes, then, represent necessary *attitudes* of

mind and spirit. "Blessed are the poor in spirit: for theirs is the kingdom of heaven." I'll wager that does not mean much to the average man in its King James translation. Goodspeed is clearer: "Blessed are those who feel their *spiritual need* . . ." The riches of the kingdom of heaven cannot possibly be given to the man who is so satisfied with his smug little self that he feels no need of anything more. It would be like casting pearls before swine. After all, a pig has no conception of the value of beautiful pearls; he would only eat them! So, why give them to him?

Here is a little gem of a story from Jesus's lips illustrating the meaning of this first Beatitude:

"Two men went up into the temple to pray; the one a Pharisee, and the other a publican. The Pharisee stood and prayed thus with himself, God, I thank thee, that I am not as other men are, extortioners, unjust, adulterers, or even as this publican. I fast twice in the week, I give tithes of all that I possess. And the publican, standing afar off, would not lift up so much as his eyes unto heaven, but smote upon his breast, saying, God be merciful to me a sinner. I tell you, this man went down to his house justified rather than the other: for every one that exalteth himself shall be abased; and he that humbleth himself shall be exalted." (Luke 18: 10–14.)

The publican's need was deep and haunting and so his prayer was answered. When we experience an inner lack, we are to ask and seek and knock: "For every one that asketh receiveth; and he that seeketh findeth; and to him that knocketh it shall be opened" (Matt. 7:8).

Ever notice how mysteriously the right thing is thrust at you at a critical moment of deep need when the heart is blindly reaching out for help? Calling in a certain home one day, I met a cleaning woman who was there doing her regular Thursday clean-up job. There was strength and radiance in her otherwise rugged and rather homely face. When I was introduced to her she put down her mop pail and sat down for a rest. She was a widow with three small children to support on fifty cents an hour. "A month ago I got to feeling that the battle to keep my home together might soon prove too much for me," she said. "I was sitting at home at the end of a hard day, about ready to throw in the sponge, when I picked up the evening paper and saw this." She reached into an apron pocket and handed me a clipping:

> I'm bruised and battered and beaten
>   Though life has urged me to win.
> But count me not as defeated,
>   For this moment again I begin.

"God must have sent me that at the critical moment," she said, "because all I have to do when I feel low is to read it, and away I go again." She is one of the blessed who "feel their spiritual need."

"Blessed are they that mourn: for they shall be comforted." Mourning for a departed loved one is not a thing that any of us would choose; but soon or late it comes to us all. Through our blinding tears, we ask the most searching questions for perhaps the first time in our lives. "Why, O

God? Where is my loved one now? What is the meaning of this mystery called death? Did Jesus actually vanquish this enemy, and shall I see my beloved again if I am counted worthy?" Such are the anguished cries of those that mourn; and if we come running to our Heavenly Father, as little children run to their earthly fathers in time of trouble, we shall be comforted; the roots of our lives will sink deeper into the soil of certainty, and we shall be stronger people when time has healed the hurt.

"Blessed are the meek: for they shall inherit the earth." Will they? The world does not commonly accept this teaching as realistic. Goodspeed's translation is more accurate: "Blessed are the humble-minded . . ." Life is deeper than logic, and the universe has seldom been known to give her prizes into the hands of the arrogant. Scientists advise their pupils to sit down humbly before their data if they would search out secrets. The Pilgrim Fathers were a humble-minded group in England searching out the Spirit of God in their own ways. An arrogant King and Parliament drove them from the land, but they ended up possessing the greatest land on earth! The Nazis despised the humble-minded. They worshiped only supermen who knew it all. The crash of their world dream of conquest was sure and complete. Likewise, the destruction of the opinionated Soviet empire is only a matter of time. "What doth the Lord require of thee, but to do justly, and to love mercy, and to walk *humbly* with thy God?" The pages of history are dotted with proof: "Blessed are the humble-minded; for they shall inherit the earth."

"Blessed are they which do hunger and thirst after righteousness: for they shall be filled." The word "righteousness" is a stumbling block to many. What young person would admit to be hungry for *that*? But Goodspeed's more accurate "uprightness" puts this Beatitude in a different light. We all ought to hunger for that. Lack of it will ruin any life; and it is a safe assumption that the men in high positions of government whose names have been connected with scandal in recent years could heartily wish that they had demonstrated uprightness instead of craven venality.

The late Lou Gehrig was the idol of millions of boys. He was one of the all-time greats in baseball. Then suddenly he was forced to retire from the game because of an incurable creeping paralysis. When two positions were offered to him he took the $6,000 one as parole commissioner of New York City instead of the $30,000 one. The latter would have entailed the use of his name over a large and popular restaurant and drinking place. He said: "It didn't seem the right thing to do. I wouldn't actually have had anything to do with it in the first place; and somehow I didn't want my name in lights over a place like that." "Blessed are those who hunger and thirst after uprightness, for they shall be satisfied." If you could page Lou Gehrig in the other world to which he has gone, do you not think he would testify that he is satisfied with the choice he made? If the lure of gold had caused him to sanction the use of his name above a drinking place, and some of the boys who worshiped him had taken their first drinks there, could a man like Lou Gehrig ever have forgiven himself?

"Blessed are the merciful: for they shall obtain mercy." Jesus was surrounded by self-righteous churchmen who were so intent upon saving themselves by observing the letter of the law that they had no time or inclination to show forth the quality of mercy toward their less punctilious brothers. They were the kind who would pull an ox from a ditch on the Sabbath, because it would otherwise have cost them money; but those same "holy" men denounced the Master for healing a man on the Sabbath, because that was "work" and hence a breaking of the law of Moses! Mercy for the sick! It never entered their selfish minds.

In *The Wingless Victory*, Maxwell Anderson has written a tragedy that should be read by every churchman in the world. The scene is Salem, Massachusetts, about the year 1800. Nathaniel McQueston and his wife, Oparre, are the central characters. He is a sea captain who left Salem in poverty to return wealthy. Meanwhile Oparre, a Malay princess, has saved his life, they have fallen in love and have married. When they finally return to Salem with their two children they meet the bitter rebuff of a racial prejudice that is all the more bitter because of the covetous spirit of the self-righteous who envied the captain his possessions.

Oparre, a worshiper of the tribal gods of revenge and blood, has been drawn to the gentle, loving Christ. She tries to use Christ's love and understanding to win the friendship of her husband's people; but they are cruel in their intolerance even when they hear her say, "Still carrying in my heart the secret Christ by whom you love, I answer, I am your friend." But she warns them, "Dark as your words have been, dark as your looks at me . . . your evil is as the play of children to the world we two have left behind us."

Even so, they will have none of her, nor her children. They would ruin her husband. At last she speaks to her husband's brother, a clergyman whose prejudice is the more terrible because of his passion for religion: "Sir, if this winter coast is tarnished by our footsteps in the snow, as I feared it might be; if the Christ you worship gives sanctuary only to his own lest they be polluted, say this at once, and we shall rouse the children, and be away. I came only with a hope."

They have their way with her, and in a moment of great trial, her husband gives way before the pressure of the community. Taking her two children with her, she repudiates Christ and turns back to her tribal gods with a broken heart. She boards a ship, resolves to die and take her babes with her. We hear her say after taking the poison and awaiting death: "God of the lesser children of the earth, the black, the unclean, the vengeful, you are mine now as when I was a child. He came too soon, this Christ of peace. Men are not ready yet. Another hundred thousand years they must drink your potion of tears and blood." *

Another hundred thousand years to wait before churchmen shall start demonstrating love and mercy to the people whose color and racial background differs from theirs? No,

* Maxwell Anderson, *The Wingless Victory* (Washington: Anderson House, 1936), pp. 51, 52, 125–126.

the leaven of Christ's teaching is changing our social climate at a dizzy rate these days.

"Blessed are the pure in heart: for they shall see God." Purity, as Jesus uses the word here, means much more than freedom from the bondage of too much sex imagery. In its full and complete sense, purity is recognizing God alone as the one supreme Cause of all that is beautiful and true and good, and the only real Power in existence. It means about the same thing as the singleness of eye to which Jesus referred in "If therefore thine eye be *single*, thy whole body shall be full of light." The single eye—the mind that beholds the love, poise, and healing peace of God so resolutely and so completely that it leaves no room for negative thinking—is the Master Key to the abundant life. It is nothing less than a technique of spiritual living calculated to banish fear, want, illness, and limitation.

This Beatitude could be stated in the forms: Blessed are they who recognize God as the only real Presence and Power in the universe; who keep their minds so centered on him that all evil and negation cease to exist, and vanish into the nothingness whence they came; who comprehend the *Law of the Universe: As Within So Without.*

"Blessed are the peacemakers: for they shall be called the children of God!" These are they who bring about peace or serenity in their own souls by practicing the preceding principles of life and hence become demonstrators of peace to others. These are heirs of the Kingdom and sons of God. The silent thought and the single eye of All-Power, of Love and Wisdom are trouble solvents of magic proportions and bringers of real peace. "Peace I leave with you, my peace I give unto you . . . let not your heart be troubled, neither let it be afraid." No wonder Jesus called such people blessed or happy! Sons of God!

The last two blessed of the eight-notched key to the happy life may be considered together: "Blessed are those who have endured persecution for their uprightness, for the Kingdom of Heaven belongs to them." "*Blessed are you when people abuse you and persecute you and falsely say everything bad of you, on my account. Be glad and exult over it, for you will be richly rewarded in heaven, for that is the way they persecuted the prophets which went before you.*"

You see, dear friends, "the proof of the pudding is in the eating." Jesus is saying that if we really practice the principles of the good life he has been describing, and keep on practicing them in the face of persecution, ridicule, and trouble, we shall demonstrate that they work even there, and our inner satisfaction and happiness shall know no bounds. They shall be found to work under any and all conditions. Isaiah, Jeremiah, Amos, and other prophets had suffered great persecution hundreds of years before Jesus's day, but they were still the most influential voices on the landscape; they were very much alive. Jesus is saying: "Follow these life principles, and you will be as deathless as they; you will be immortal; you will be Sons of the Living God!"

Silent Communion for Using the Eight-Notched Key

√ **The light of God surrounds me;**
The love of God infolds me;
The power of God protects me;
The presence of God watches over me;
Wherever I am, God is! *

* An affirmation used by the Unity School of Christianity in Lee's Summit, Mo. Used by permission.

CHAPTER TEN

The Secret Weapon

"Ye have heard that it hath been said, An eye for an eye, and a tooth for a tooth: But I say unto you, That ye resist not evil: but whosoever shall smite thee on thy right cheek, turn to him the other also. . . . And whosoever shall compel thee to go a mile, go with him twain." (Matt. 5:38–39, 41.)

Jesus was the most revolutionary of all teachers. His insights were deeper and truer than those of any who have preceded or followed him. He was well versed in the old Mosaic law, which was, in spots, crude and barbarous. Exodus 21:23–25 enjoined upon the Hebrews the taking of "life for life, eye for eye, tooth for tooth, foot for foot, hand for hand, burning for burning, wound for wound, stripe for stripe." That rough-and-ready justice was better than none, perhaps, but it was no way to settle a dispute with any hope of permanence.

Both participants to such an ordeal were left worse off than before the "settlement." The man whose tooth or eye was knocked out in retaliation was angrier than before, while the man who knocked it out was brutalized in the process. As Booker T. Washington once said, "You can't hold a man in a ditch without getting down there yourself." Jesus was primarily interested in motives. In Matthew 5:22, what Jesus condemned was not the calling of a man a "fool" but the *anger* that caused the outburst. If a man, feeling very pious, started down the aisle with a gift for the altar and suddenly remembered that he was angry with a neighbor, he was directed to put the gift down then and there and go out and settle his misunderstanding; then he was to come back, pick up his gift, and present it to God.

And how must a man proceed with such a business? By forgiving his brother up to seventy times seven or an indefinite number of times. This sets the brother free; you loose him and let him go, for thus only can you free yourself of the destructive poisons of anger and bitterness. To return evil for evil and hatred for hatred is to start a vicious circle to which there is no end short of the destruction of the enemy *and of one's self.*

"Ye have heard that it hath been said, Thou shalt love thy neighbour, and hate thine enemy. But I say unto you, Love your enemies, bless them that curse you, do good to them that hate you, and pray for them which despitefully use you, and persecute you; that ye may be the children of your Father which is in heaven: for he maketh his sun to rise on the evil and on the good, and sendeth rain on the just and on the unjust." (Matt. 5:43–45.) Do you see the splendid but simple technique involved here? *Pray for them!* When we turn our minds to the God of Light, Truth, and Love and hold our enemy in that Presence, something wonderful happens to us as well as to him; our own self-pride and littleness comes into sharp focus, and we are forced to admit our share of the blame. The high, accusing pitch is toned out of the voice, the piercing, gimlet quality recedes from the eye, we gain control of ourselves. We are then in a position to give the soft answer that turns away wrath; we have a friend instead of an enemy, and we have automatically stepped onto higher ground and *taken our brother with us*!

Here is no doctrine for weaklings. This new and revolutionary teaching was a direct challenge to the best and finest in the souls of all men. It was a pattern of life well calculated to solve the vexatious relationships between the hated Roman rulers and the helpless, subject Hebrews. If a Roman forces you to carry his baggage a mile, said Jesus, have the graciousness to carry on for still another mile. The first mile was enjoined by Roman law. The second mile was enjoined by Jesus. Wherever tried, it produced magic results; but most people did not have the inner controls to try it. They simply were not big enough. Jesus noted this and told the Jewish people that failure to step onto the high plateau of Christlike living would cause the violent end of that age. Not one stone would be left on top of another in the Temple. Hatred begets only hatred and destruction. His prophecy came true in A.D. 70 when Titus took Jerusalem, completely destroyed the great Temple, and dispersed the Jews.

The pages of history are covered with the records of men who went down to dusty, ignominious death because they refused to accept or countenance the use of Jesus's Secret Weapon of Constructive Nonresistance to Evil, or overcoming evil with good. Look at the Nazis. Hitler's childhood and youth were full of misery and frustration. He loved his mother and hated his tyrannical father. Sickly in body, he was a failure in the public schools. He tried the art school and was rejected because of insufficient talent. When his mother died he drifted to Vienna, where he lived for a time in a charitable institution maintained through the generosity of a Jew. He remained in Vienna for some years, loafing and adrift for the most part, but doing occasional odd jobs such as carrying luggage from the railroad station, shoveling snow, painting houses, and decorating postcards. Gradually poverty, ill health, the loss of his mother, obscurity, unemployment, hunger, neglect, and the frustration of his dream of becoming an artist festered in his sickly personality until he began to look upon himself as the symbol of an oppressed but defiant humanity.

In this mood he returned to Munich after the German defeat in 1918. He painted some pictures and took them to an art museum to be exhibited. The committee looked over his work and turned him down. On his way out, he asked the porter the names of the committee. When he learned that three of the five were Jews, he gnashed his teeth, shook his fist in their direction, and cried, "I'll be back." In August of 1939, just as the war was breaking and the Nazi legions were gathering on the Polish border, I was in Munich. The day before my arrival, Hitler had grandly opened a new art museum costing millions of dollars. I wondered how he felt he could spare the time to journey from Berlin for the dedication of an art museum at such an hour of crisis. Then I learned the story recounted above. He had had the old museum torn down and a new one built in its place. His vow was kept. He had "come back."

Gradually, the temper of the beaten, frustrated German people had risen so that Adolf Hitler with his "victory through hatred" philosophy could rise to power. Ernst Röhm, Gregor Strasser, Baldur von Schirach, Alfred Rosenberg, Göring, Goebbels, and others were ready to become his supergangsters. As the Nazi movement grew, the little Austrian corporal (he was not admitted to German citizenship until 1932) became the voice of frustrated Germany. Down with the lesser breeds of the human family—the Russians, the Poles, the Czechs, the Hungarians, the Croats, the Jews! Down with the Christianity that sprang from weak Jewish sources! Down with treaties that tied the superior Teutons to the past! Does the world doubt that superiority? Then it shall be demonstrated in the "supreme test of battle."

Looking around for an intellectually respectable philosophical basis for the new doctrines, the Nazis found a philosopher ready-made for their needs: Friedrich Wilhelm Nietzsche. On my desk is a fascinating book entitled *Nietzsche* by Crane Brinton of Harvard. In that book is a photograph that Hitler once ordered taken showing himself as pupil gazing fondly at Nietzsche the master in the Nietzsche-Archiv in Weimar.

Let us have a brief look at this strange and contradictory

man. When Nietzsche was seven years old his pastor father died and left him to be brought up by four women: his mother, grandmother, and two aunts. He was weak in body and suffered constantly from irritating headaches and weak eyes. He was the laughingstock of his playmates, this squint-eyed "little minister" with the enormous head stuck on a diminutive body. He was afraid of other boys. He envied them and their strength, their ability to play roughly and to use slang that he, with his superior knowledge of books, seemed to be unable to use. Thus, despising himself, he lapsed into a dream life where he could fight ferocious battles and shed oceans of blood without suffering the pain from which his sensitive nature shrank.

Gradually he cut himself loose from the Christian faith. He came to think it was a religion for weaklings. It taught renunciation of the pleasures of the senses. He thought that was a denial of life. Unable to conquer by the sword, early churchmen had ruled by "piety and prayer." They taught the dignity of the timid and the glory of the weak—"all of this to shackle the natural instincts of the strong." Christianity "is the most pious fraud in history," said Nietzsche.

In *Thus Spake Zarathustra*, his philosophy is most plainly stated: "Blood is the spirit of man. Of all that is written, I love only what a man hath written with his blood . . . Be not ashamed of the hatred and the envy within your hearts. It is glorious to hate and to be envious . . . it is the good war that halloweth every cause . . . Be strong. Be unafraid. I command you to laugh at what little men call sin. You who proclaim the ego as something holy and divine shall openly avow that selfishness, voluptuousness, and passion for power are the true virtues of manhood . . . I hear the voice of a new and greater and more individualistic race of men—*the voice of their will to power.*"

Hitler deliberately dethroned Christ and enthroned Nietzsche. He unloosed a flood of hate that swept over the ramparts of Europe destroying everything in its path, *including the Nazis.* As Jesus said: "The stone which the builders rejected, the same is become the head of the corner . . . And whosoever shall fall on this stone shall be broken: but on whomsoever it shall fall, it will grind him to powder." (Matt. 21:42, 44.)

Does this teaching of nonresistance mean that we should not build up a strong defense system to hold in check the onward march of world Communism? I think not. If there were no strong air, sea, and land forces to oppose them the masters of the Kremlin would, without a single doubt, take over control of the earth. All potential opposition leaders in America, Britain, and other free lands would be executed or worked to death in forced labor camps; our children would be trained in the brutal Marxist philosophy of life and become lost to freedom, Christianity, and democracy. Something far worse than the Dark Ages would be our universal lot.

Deplorable though it be, we seem to have no alternative to building up our armed forces. This would appear to be our only hope of avoiding a third world war. But this is not enough; not by a long shot! This is not Constructive Nonresistance. In my judgment, we must go on rapidly to revamp the United Nations into a limited Federal World Government with power to make, interpret, and enforce world law to prevent war. In addition, we must expand the so-called Point Four program of our government until we are helping many more millions of poverty-stricken masses of the world to a higher standard of life. Only thus will they turn a deaf ear to the false Pied Pipers of the Communist world.

Someone may now ask why we call this a *Secret Weapon.* Jesus said: "When thou prayest, enter into thy closet, and when thou hast shut thy door, pray to thy Father which is in secret; and thy Father which seeth in secret shall reward thee openly" (Matt. 6:6). There is to be no boasting, no talk about the thing we are going to do. In the silence and aloneness of the secret place, we talk to the Father and ask that our hearts may replace evil with goodness, falsehood with truth, and hatred with love. We visualize ourselves, with the help of God, quietly confronting the enemy with poise, forgiveness, understanding, and unbreakable good will. This is overcoming evil with good. This is constructive nonresistance. This is our secret weapon against which the enemy is quite helpless.

Let us not allow literalism to rob us of our secret weapon. Let us not say that we cannot see a red-blooded man turning the other cheek. When they struck Jesus in the face at his trial (Luke 22:64), he did not turn the other cheek. He endured their insults with superb dignity and self-control. When Branch Rickey told Jackie Robinson that he had in mind signing him to the Dodgers but that Jackie, as the first colored player in the big leagues, would be provoked to wrath again and again, he went on to say: "Tell me, What will you do when someone, without provocation, hauls off and hits you in the face?" Jackie said: "I have another cheek—isn't that right, Mr. Rickey?" And he did just that. He used this secret weapon to win over an implacable opposition. Today the big leagues have plenty of colored boys as a result of Jackie's magnificent conduct.

Dr. Robert R. Moton knew what that fight was. Following his graduation from Hampton Institute in 1890, this great Negro educator was associated with that school for twenty-five years. He was baffled and frustrated and humiliated again and again by the unreasoning racial prejudice that he experienced everywhere, even among white people whose names were high on some church roll. But he believed that the only way by which his people could advance was by showing the understanding, forgiving, loving spirit of Christ even in the face of the severest provocation.

Later, when he had become the president of Tuskegee Institute, he was riding on a train when an arrogant white man said in a loud voice, "Hey, boy, fetch me a drink of water." Dr. Moton could have replied: "Do you know to whom you are speaking? I am Dr. Moton, a Ph.D. and head of a great educational institution. If you want a drink, you will find water at the end of the car."

Instead, he used the technique of a Christian gentleman. He arose without a word and smilingly brought the man some water. Then he introduced himself and engaged the white brother in conversation. At the end of an hour he had made a lifelong friend for Tuskegee who would one day bring financial assistance desperately needed.

Years later a crisis developed at the school. When the government built a large Negro veterans' hospital the white people of Tuskegee demanded that it be staffed entirely by white doctors, but Dr. Moton insisted that part of the staff should be Negroes. A mob of whites called at his home and threatened his life one night unless he would give in. He walked quietly out onto his front porch and faced them. "All my life," he said, "has been based on a belief in the tolerance, the humanity, and the ultimate fairness of the white man. Without that, my life has no meaning; if it is violated, it is better that my life should end."

This courageous stand so won the sympathy of his neighbors that he carried the day on the hospital staff; and the next year the Spingarn medal was awarded to him for outstanding service in the cause of better race relations.

Don't be discouraged because you have tried to demonstrate this magnificent control and failed. So have we all! The fault has been ours, of course, through our failure to spend enough time in the secret closet. One experience of the successful use of the weapon, however, will give such a warm and satisfying glow inside us that we shall be impelled to try it again and yet again. A glorious unfoldment of new spiritual power will be our reward. So, use the following affirmation to feed the deep mind with the raw materials of success.

Silent Communion for Overcoming Evil with Good

"He that dwelleth in the secret place of the most High shall abide under the shadow of the Almighty. I will say of the Lord, He is my refuge and my fortress: my God; in him will I trust." (Psalm 91:1–2.)

Night and day, never ceasing, I am dwelling in the secret place of the most High, filling my whole mind with the Beauty, Truth, Radiance, and Love of God. Against this All-Power, evil has no chance, and I am thanking God constantly for this Cosmic Truth.

CHAPTER ELEVEN

Flame Up and Shine

The Nazis inflicted just about every form of indignity upon Philippe Vernier because he was a man of peace. They placed him in a filthy prison without cause, and starved his fine little family. But an American officer who called upon him afterwards reported that the visit with this luminous soul was the high-water mark of his life and that this gentleman was "incorrigibly Christian."

Read this beautiful letter from Vernier's hand:

"If you are a disciple of the Master, it is up to you to illume the earth. You do not have to groan over everything the world lacks; *you are there to bring it what it needs.*

"There where reign hatred, malice, and discord you will put love, pardon, and peace. For lying you will bring truth; for despair, hope; for doubt, faith; there where is sadness you will give joy. If you are in the smallest degree the servant of God, all these virtues of light you will carry within you.

"Do not be frightened by a mission so vast! It is not really you who are charged with the fulfillment of it. You are only the *torch-bearer.* The fire, even if it burns within you, even when it burns you, is never lit by you. It uses you as it uses the oil of the lamp. You hold it, feed it, carry it around; but it is the fire that works, that gives light to the world, and to yourself at the same time.

"*Your faith, your love, and the joy that enlivens you are only lent to you. All these might be taken away; all the more reason for spreading them widely. You do not know how long you will keep the flame. In the meantime send out the greatest possible radiance! Do not be the clogged lantern that chokes and smothers the light; the lamp, timid or ashamed, hidden under a bushel. Flame up and shine before men; lift high the fire of God.*"

Jesus called his followers "the light of the world" and commanded them to let their light shine in order to glorify their Father in heaven. Light is quiet and life-giving. When light is shining, darkness is automatically absent. There is no struggle, no noise. When the sun heaves his giant, yellow shoulders over the eastern horizon, the darkness does not stop to contest his coming. It dissolves in the magic solvent of the new radiance and quietly ceases to be.

The world is full of baffled and troubled people. Two world wars seem not to have settled anything. Another world war might possibly be looming on the far horizon. Divorces mount, mental hospitals overflow, drunkenness increases, and millions wander in the labyrinthine corridors of confusion and despair. What can one man do?

Flame up and shine! says Philippe Vernier. Don't struggle too long with the problem of evil until you have wrestled with the problem of goodness. Did you ever try to explain

Jesus? How did it come about that he lived his life of loving service, shining in this dark world like a flaming sun, and then went out praying for those who put him to death? Can you explain that?

There is only one possible explanation of the problem of goodness. Jesus but radiated the source of his light, which was in God. For lying, he brought truth; for despair, hope; for doubt, faith; for sadness, joy. He did not spend much time lamenting the past nor worrying about the future. He was a specialist in the Eternal Now. You are the light of the world, now; let your light shine before men, now, and the rest will take care of itself. For those with a living, pulsing faith in the loving Father whose kingdom is within, it is possible to flame up and shine and to make of today a memorable occasion. If you do not have this God-consciousness, dare to start acting as if you had it, and see where you come out!

New York is a notoriously impersonal city in spite of its millions. But that is where Salvatore Cascavilla has been shining for a long, long time. Emigrating from Italy a quarter of a century ago, he has worked up to the job of driving a heavy green and yellow bus. His customers call him Singing Sam because he is so sunny and polite and kind.

To the man who was worrying about getting to the Pennsylvania Station in time to catch a certain train, Sam said: "Now, just sit back and catch your breath and take it easy. We get there six minutes ahead of train time, but I'll speed up a little so you won't have to hurry." That man later sent a check made out to "The Most Courteous Bus

Driver in New York," and Sam's bank honored it without question.

The first part of Sam's run is through Harlem, where his unfailing good nature has won him hosts of colored friends. "Good morning," he beams, "and how are *you* this fine morning? . . . A transfer? Yes, sir! With pleasure!" As he rolls along, shopkeepers, policemen, taxi drivers, and children wave to him. As an old Negro preacher put it: "Sam has done a lot for the colored people on his run in the last nine years. There couldn't be a finer sermon than the one he preaches every day."

When a customer gets off, Sam calls out some such remark as: "Got to go so soon? Well, have a happy day. Come back again. Goodbye." When a taxi driver, trying to beat a yellow light, shot out of a side street directly in front of Sam and gave vent to a string of curdling oaths when the bus stopped, Sam calmly leaned out and said, "Thank you, son, for stopping so quickly," and the argument never materialized.

He sings so much because "it seems to make everybody feel better—kind of loosens them up and makes them hum and whistle too. That's good for you." And a New York doctor who rides with him agrees. He says a fifteen-minute ride with Sam every morning is his indispensable morning tonic—better than medicine. He even thinks Sam may be happily keeping some people away from the doctor. When an elderly colored woman was running to catch the bus Sam pulled up, opened the door, and shouted: "Don't run. I'll wait. People your age should never run—bad for the heart. Take your time now—we'll wait till you get your seat."

Sam has been written up many times in newspapers and magazines as a rare specimen because he is always dispensing sunshine—and that in spite of the fact he had a crippled and bedridden wife for many years. But why should this be such a rare phenomenon? Should we not all be doing it every hour of every day? Could we not all make life much easier for ourselves and for every living soul who comes within the hourly radius of our lives?

Only yesterday I caught myself rushing down the street toward a Kiwanis Club luncheon. Suddenly I stopped and reflected, What's your hurry? Here I was, rushing along without a glance at the shining sun in the blue-arched dome of heaven or at the fresh new green of the grass after last night's shower, without any regard for the creative miracle of the trees just beginning to put on their new green dresses. It seems to me that most of us miss the joy of life when we fail to extract the maximum of pleasure from each passing moment. Thus we have nothing to spill over into the lives of others.

This is the lesson that Gontran de Poncins learned. He had been thirty days on the trail with an Eskimo family with the temperature sometimes hitting 50 below. As they pushed steadily forward through the snow and the cold he kept asking, "How many days is it to King William Land?" The Eskimo father, however, would never commit himself. He seemed to feel they were doing all right, and that it did not matter when they would arrive.

Finally the repeated question seemed to get under the Eskimo's skin. He walked over and studied his white friend's face for some time. "Don't the dogs go as well as you would like?" he asked. At that the mother and child also looked at him, and even the dogs turned their heads as they stood in their traces. There was silence, and Eskimos have a way of giving weight to silence. "Isn't that sled a good sled?" the man continued. "Aren't you glad that the snow over the sea is lasting through our journey?"

At that moment Poncins learned a lesson that he never forgot: "The stone age with its simplicity and the Orient with its wisdom were looking at me and trying to get me to understand. 'Why hurry?' they said. 'And where is it that you are always wanting to be going? Why concern yourself with the future when the present is so magnificent?' " *

To think of the past is often to regret it. To think of the future is to fear it. But the present! Is that not the only understandable reality? The world is surely what the mind makes it. Even the Arctic was not a heartbreaking place to the Eskimos, but a great empire of ice and snow of which they were the kings.

The Iowa State Highway Commission frequently puts up, beside the road where someone has been killed, a sign bearing the word "Think!" in heavy black letters, and a ragged red cross beneath it symbolizing the life that has been snuffed out. Sometimes three or four of these ominous

* Gontran de Poncins and Lewis Galantiere, *Kabloona* (New York: Reynal & Hitchcock, 1941).

warnings stand together indicating the seriousness of the moment in the past when failure to think caused the sacrifice of a number of precious lives. *Think!* Don't try to pass another car on a curve or a hill. *Think!* Don't approach that blind intersection at seventy miles an hour!

Think! But don't limit your thinking to the matter of staying alive. *Think!* Try to discover what significance this day has in the total business of living. What is it you really want from life? What are your real aims and ambitions, and does your fevered rush through the days have any permanent and worth-while meaning?

Golden Boy is a play everyone ought to see, and it is good to have it in motion picture form. Clifford Odets has something to say that should stop us in our tracks. Joe is a promising young Italian violinist. He knows that his music pulls at people's heartstrings and sends them out of the concert hall subdued, smiling, and thoughtful, enriching both the artist and all who listen. But he is not happy. There is neither the fame nor the riches in his creative gift that he sees coming to boys in the prize ring; boys without artistic gifts, who have plenty of brawn and muscle and a peculiar ability to smash their way through to one knockout victory after another; boys who make tens of thousands of dollars a year and fill the sport pages of the newspapers with their photographs. Money and fame! That is what Golden Boy must have!

So, he gives up his violin for the gloves. His overweening ambition and brawn make him a savage fighter, and he becomes a sensation. Even when he makes love to the woman he idolizes, he shouts and curses at the least indication that she is not wholly subservient to his wishes. Even when he breaks his precious hand and forever cuts himself off from any return to his true career, he is not dismayed. Nervous, loud-mouthed, and bombastic, he strides on to his final doom. Sitting in the theater, one is tempted to shout: "*Think!* Golden Boy, think! Don't be a fool! The fact that there is no light, no joy, no living flame in your life should warn you that you are following a dream with neither substance nor reality. Slow down! Think! Give the inner splendor in your immortal soul a chance to shine!"

If we are to flame up and shine as Vernier suggests, we must have a light within. That light is not kindled by great possessions or by hurrying from one place to another. It is not kindled by our advancement into high position. The smoldering embers of life are blown into flame by the daring act of faith that links our little lives to the Central Light of the World—God. Then even adversity but fans the flames to greater strength. For hatred, malice, and discord, we substitute love and pardon and peace; for lying, truth; for despair, hope; for doubt, faith; and for sadness, joy.

A Christian traveler has once told of his strange discovery one day in a little village whose traditions date from the sixteenth century. He arrived toward evening, as the church bell rang. The edifice was shadowed and dark, but from every byway came worshipers, each bearing a bronze lamp of very old design. Joining the throng, the traveler asked about the lamps and received the answer: "We have no other way of lighting our church. In the year 1550, when it was built, the seigneur of the village decided that each attendant should carry his lamp. The lamps belong to the church, which lends them to the people. We light them at a torch as we enter."

"And," asked the stranger, "that does not keep people from attending the evening service?"

"*Not at all, monsieur. Our church is known as the church of the lighted lamps. Each one comes to make it more bright, for he knows that if he stays at home, the church will be the darker for it and the service more somber.* The pastor must have before him every lighted lamp and each dark spot speaks of one absent."

"Let your light so shine before men," said Jesus, "that they may see your good works, and glorify your Father which is in heaven." And where is heaven? It should be within us. "The kingdom of heaven is within you," said the Master. So God is never far away.

I love the story of the Indian lad who at the tender age of seven, taking only a bow and arrow, went out alone into the dark woods one night with instructions to prove that he was now worthy of receiving his first initiation into manhood. With fear and trembling he went into the darkness to search for a chance to prove that he was now a man. Tense with excitement, he quaked at every unexpected sound. At long last he was overjoyed to note the first pale streaks of dawn of a new day. A twig snapped behind a tree, and he nervously raised and stretched his bow, only to discover his own father standing there. The father had kept the long night vigil close by him, ready to sustain him in case of need.

In these dark days, my friends, why should not we all flame up and shine? Said John of Jesus: "In him was life; and the life was the light of men. And the light shineth in darkness; and the darkness comprehended it not."

Look to this Day, for it is Life—
The very Life of Life!
In its brief course lie all the verities
And Realities of your Existence:
The Bliss of Growth,
The Glory of Action,
The Splendor of Beauty;
For Yesterday is but a dream,
And Tomorrow is only a Vision;
But Today well lived
Makes every Yesterday a Dream of Happiness,
And every Tomorrow a Vision of Hope.
Look well, therefore, to this day! *

* "The Salutation of the Dawn"—from the Sanscrit.

Silent Communion for Appropriating the Light of God

"God is light, and in him is no darkness at all" (I John 1:5).

"In him [Jesus] was life; and the life was the light of men" (John 1:4).

"Let your light shine before men" (Matt. 5:16).

The light and love of the Living God is aflame within me at this moment as I contemplate the priceless treasure of the Eternal Presence within, guiding, sustaining, and healing me.

CHAPTER TWELVE

Here Is Harmony

The word "harmony" does not appear anywhere in the entire Bible; but the word "whole" does, and it means the same thing. When a sick woman with great faith touched the hem of Jesus's garment she was healed of her long-standing infirmity, and Jesus said: "Daughter, thy faith hath made thee *whole*; go in peace" (Mark 5:34). A well body is "at ease" while an ill one suffers "disease." A whole or harmonious person is one whose body, mind, and spirit are in tune with the infinite, as the Creator intended they should be.

The whole universe was made for harmony. When one part of it gets off balance, adjustments are made automatically. The average rainstorm or snowfall is nature's attempt to restore harmony to a section that is too dry. If it sometimes seems to be overdone, a closer look may disclose that the subsurface water level is down. Even earthquakes are necessary, though violent, attempts to redress an unbalanced condition of the earth's crust.

Agricultural experts know when some pest endangers

crops that there is a harmony restorer somewhere if they can find it. It was recently announced, for example, that the European corn borer which destroyed $353,000,000 worth of corn in 1949 was able to destroy only $85,000,000 worth in 1950. A fly named *Lydella stabulans grisescens* was brought in and turned loose. She does no harm to crops and attacks no insect but the corn borer. The females tenderly place their infant maggots at the entrances of the corn borers' tunnels. The maggots, guided by the genius of their kind, crawl into the tunnels, find the borers, and destroy them by devouring them!

The greatest disharmony in the universe is among men. There is world-wide dissension and unrest. The international tension has never been greater. In our own country graft and corruption are ever present. Why? Because, I believe, we couple selfishness with a fundamental disrespect for our neighbors. Millions do not seem to care what happens to the other fellow as long as they get theirs.

Jesus said that love of God and of one's neighbor were absolutely essential to a harmonious life. The most precious value in the universe is the human personality. We all are made in the image of God with souls that are destined to live on into the countless years of God. "Reverence for Life is the key to harmony," says Dr. Albert Schweitzer.

This was depicted in Jesus's parable of the wicked husbandmen in Matthew 21:33–44. The owner of a fine vineyard rented it out to certain husbandmen and then took a long journey. At harvest time he sent his servants to collect the rent; but the husbandmen beat them up and sent them away empty-handed. This happened twice. Then the owner sent his son, saying: "They will *reverence* my son." But they killed him, thinking they could seize his inheritance. The lord of the vineyard then destroyed the wicked husbandmen and rented his vineyard to others. Jesus is saying that the law of the jungle, the law of tooth and claw, the philosophy that disregards the rights of others is the cause of disharmony and disaster in the relationships of men. He declared that the only harmony we shall ever have will come only from obeying the principles laid down in the Sermon on the Mount, the Golden Rule, the Beatitudes, and the great Commandment enjoining the love of God and of all of our neighbors, regardless of race or creed. His teaching is the starkest realism. It is good religion, and it is good common sense. It *works*, as any intelligent person can attest by becoming informed about what is going on in this world.

In 1889 Willoughby M. McCormick started a spice and flavoring extract business in Baltimore. By 1928 he had a three and a half million dollar business. A hard-boiled boss, he considered his men as so many "hands," and any back talk or complaints from them resulted in instant dismissal. The only exception to that rule was in the person of his nephew, Charles P. McCormick. Charles was fired seven times; but he had "ideas," and so the old man always hired him back.

At the bottom of the depression in 1932, McCormick & Company began losing money. Uncle Willoughby slashed wages again and again. Nephew Charles told him his packaging ideas were obsolete; his men were disgruntled and insecure in their jobs, and the company headed for the rocks. Then Willoughby died, and Charles took over. Watch now what happens when a man dares to put personality values first and business second. See what comes about when an owner seeks first the kingdom of right relations and lets all the other things which most people seek come last.

Charles's first act was to call all 500 employees together. "We are close to the rocks," he told them, "but we can win out. Prices for raw materials are low; however, we've got to turn them into salable products at lower production expense. If you'll increase production we can cut costs, lower prices, and thus give our salesmen the stimulus they need to bring in orders. That means an all-out effort on your part, and you can't do it on poor pay and long hours. So, we are raising your pay ten per cent and reducing the work week from 48 hours to 44. *From now on every worker is going to prosper exactly as the firm prospers.*" *

The effect of this remarkable proposal was nothing short of breathtaking. With hands and hearts the employees plunged into their work. In three short months, they cut costs by eliminating waste and increasing production. The company moved out of the red about that time, and Charlie shoved wages up another notch. At the same time he instituted worker meetings with no bosses present. They were to study ways and means of devising more attractive packaging and sales methods and of eliminating every obstacle to harmonious relations and efficiency.

Recommendations poured in from these meetings, and

* *Future*, July, 1950.

many were adopted. Every worker with a grievance was encouraged to bring his trouble openly to a factory board of workers created for that purpose. They were heard by their peers. All felt a sense of dignity and worth. Fifteen-minute rest periods were put in at midmorning and afternoon. Rested employees again sent production skywards. Hours came down to forty a week as wages increased and bonuses, health insurance, and other benefits were adopted. Ways and means of eliminating the old slack season and payless lay-offs were studied until job security was finally guaranteed to every person throughout the year.

Gradually the gap between management and labor all but disappeared, and labor turnover dropped from 30 per cent to 4 per cent. Charlie McCormick not only brought a very sick business through the depression triumphantly, but built it into the largest firm of its kind in the United States. Gross sales leaped from around $2,000,000 to more than $28,000,000. And Charlie McCormick has written a book on the plan called *Power of People*.

As a matter of fact, this and similar experiments have reduced owner-employee friction so far that we find ourselves in a brand-new era. Ten years ago, 728 such plans were in effect; now the number has increased to more than 12,000. The trouble spots still get the headlines; but, all over the nation, managers and owners are eliminating disharmony by putting personality values and right relations first; and they are finding that a lowly Carpenter two thousand years ago in Nazareth knew more about how to be both successful and happy in the business world than anybody else who ever lived. He was the greatest expert in bringing harmony into human relations that the world has ever seen.

Another man who has a basic respect for all human beings regardless of race or color is J. Oliver Emmerich, editor of the McComb, Mississippi, *Enterprise-Journal.* In a little over a quarter of a century, this soft-spoken country editor has completely changed the atmosphere and living standards of the entire county, and his friendly contagion is spilling over into all surrounding areas. In 1949 the *Progressive Farmer* named him "man of the year in agriculture" for Mississippi; four times the National Editorial Association has given him awards for community service and superior editing. The United States Chamber of Commerce, the United Nations, and many people all over the South are following his work with deep interest.

He believes primarily in *helping people to help themselves rather than relying upon government handouts.* So, he raises money among businessmen to lend to poor farmers who will follow scientific procedures, as described daily in his newspaper. Enriched land in Pike County caused the corn yield to jump from 15 to 31 bushels per acre in two years. Poultry production was multiplied by ten in two years. So it went with sweet potatoes, 4-H clubs, Bang's disease control, and forestry improvement.

Emmerich is vitally interested in developing boys and girls and building them into sturdy self-reliant citizens. His grass roots program has dotted the countryside with 4-H clubs and given fine prizes for achieving outstanding results.

Take the case of Clotile Simmons. When this Negro girl

joined one of the 4-H clubs she was an eighth grader and a part-time house servant, and lived with her parents and eight brothers and sisters in a dilapidated cabin. She entered Emmerich's Happy Living contest and enlisted the enthusiastic support of her entire family. Today, they live in a modern home with electricity and running water, and they have twenty-three dairy cows and hundreds of chickens. Clotile was named over 985 other Mississippi girls for having done the state's best job in home improvement. Multiply this heartening example by several thousand, dear friends, and you can readily understand what one crusading editor has accomplished in helping vast numbers of people to attain a more abundant life. It is an example of what Jesus meant by loving your neighbor as you love yourself.

Great Britain's prestige and economic status would be much higher today if her statesmen had taken time out some time ago to reread their Bibles and had taken seriously Jesus's Golden Rule and Great Commandment. I refer to Britain's sad loss of the ill-fated Anglo-Iranian Oil Company and of the profits therefrom that she so desperately needs. She insisted on keeping 75 per cent of the profits at a time when Americans were splitting their Iranian oil income on a 50–50 basis. The highly volatile and poverty-stricken Iranians became so enraged that they finally drove out the luckless Britons entirely.

At the same time American relations with the Venezuelans are tranquil and profitable for both sides; Americans have considered the Venezuelans' needs as well as their own. The Creole Petroleum Corporation in Venezuela is owned in the United States. This enterprise is the world's number-two producer with 2,422 wells, from which 750,000 barrels of black crude oil flow daily.

Harmonious relations in this case are due to two wise policies—equality with Venezuela in profits, and genuine concern for the welfare of the personnel. Qualified Venezuelans are hired in preference to outsiders; lessons in Spanish are compulsory for all who do not know the language; housing, schools, hospitals, and cradle-to-grave welfare measures are provided for all 14,544 employees. The end result is harmony and mutual satisfaction all around.

Jesus taught that human personality is the supreme value in this universe, and that it must always be treated as supreme if we would have harmony and would truly prosper. The cold, formal, rigid religion of Jesus's day was judged on that basis and rejected. The cunningly contrived restrictions that made the observance of the Sabbath day a nightmare were swept away by one pointed sentence: "The Sabbath was made for man, not man for the Sabbath." This factual measuring rod must fit governments; governments were made for man, not man for governments, and when governments fail to respect the rights of man, they must die. Russia's government is as doomed as the dodo bird right now. Industry was made for man, not man for industry; and when industry forgets its primary reason for existence, it is on the way out. Page the Anglo-Iranian Oil Company!

Force can go a long way—for a while. It can hold things together and dominate the situation for a day or two or three; but on the fourth day it is finished. Lies and false propaganda can make people believe that black is white and white is black, for a while. Then comes the truth, and the lie is all done. Christ's teaching of truth and love and reverence for life is stark realism in a universe that was made for them. Try anything else and, in the long run, you are finished.

It is significant that after Jesus told the parable of the wicked husbandmen and their certain and tragic fate, he looked the chief priests straight in the eye and said: "Did ye never read in the scriptures, The stone which the builders rejected"—Jesus's teaching on the Great Commandment, Golden Rule and Sermon on the Mount as the only guide to harmony in human relations—"the same is become the head of the corner . . . And whosoever shall fall on this stone shall be broken: but on whomsoever it shall fall, it will grind him to powder." (Matt. 21:42, 44.)

Powerful words, those; spoken with deep conviction and finality. Put personality values first; demonstrate reverence for life through attitudes of understanding, mercy, sympathy, and love. Watch the inner splendor in a man shine forth with a steady glow when he releases it by using these creative attitudes. Use Jesus's realistic test: "By their fruits ye shall know them," in the home, factory, or playground. Do this, and experience harmony in all of life's relations. Fail to do it, and find your fondest dreams ground "to powder." Such is the realism of the Good News about God.

Silent Communion for Building Harmony Into Life

The supreme value in the universe is human personality. Jesus's command is to love my neighbor as myself; to seek first the Kingdom of Right Relationships and everything else will follow.

"Love is patient and kind. It is not rude. It does not insist on its own rights. It does not become angry. It is not resentful. It is not happy over injustice, it is only happy with truth." (I Cor. 13:4–6, Goodspeed translation.)

I am developing Harmony through kindness, sympathy, understanding, and love in every human contact. With God I cannot fail.

CHAPTER THIRTEEN

The Secret of Personal Power

In the early spring of 1935, at the bottom of the great economic depression, two hours with a little colored man gave me more insight into the secret of personal poise and power than I have ever gained through any other contact. Roland Hayes had come to Duluth to give a concert in the Armory, and Dr. A. Raymond Grant and I learned that he was not allowed to use the public dining room of his hotel. We decided to go down and apologize to him.

When we arrived at his door he was busy telephoning; but he cheerfully called out to us to come in and find seats. He flashed us a smile and waved his hand in friendly greeting as he continued his telephone conversation, and we felt immediately the warm, courteous, engaging atmosphere that his very presence creates.

He had just finished eating breakfast in his room, for the dishes were still there. So, I began the conversation by remarking that I as a Christian minister regretted exceedingly a condition in our social order that made it necessary for a colored man to stay away from public dining rooms and to enter hotels by side doors.

"There is nothing that you or any white man can do to alter that," said Mr. Hayes. "That is a job for me and my people. I am trying to live every moment with such consciousness of the Divine Presence without any trace of bitterness in my heart that that condition of prejudice and racial antipathy shall disappear. And I am trying to get my people to do likewise."

He paused and looked about the room, and smiled as he resumed. "I am perfectly happy here by myself, and nobody in all the world can hurt me except myself." Then he told of the marvelous old soul that had taught him the art of singing in his boyhood and had told him that, as a black artist, he would suffer many things if he allowed the barbs to get inside. "But always remember that, if your heart is right and your spirit divinely disciplined, nobody in all the world can hurt you."

We then asked Mr. Hayes if he had certain hours of communion and spiritual preparation for his concerts. He surprised us by saying that he did not now have such hours although years ago he had had them. "Now every breath I draw and every moment of the day is a communion with Him that is my preparation." Then he told us how he captured his audience during his first minute on the stage. "I stand there perfectly quiet with hands clasped before me and pray: that Roland Hayes may be blotted entirely out of the picture; that the people sitting there may feel only the Spirit of God flowing through melody and rhythm; that racial prejudice may be forgotten. The audience instinctively feels what is happening as I commune with my Father

—and I capture them that moment and never let them go until I am done."

From this quiet-spoken little black man an electric radiance and joy flowed around us. "What a time I have had this winter!" he said. "I have given up expensive managers and the high-priced tickets they used to insist upon. Now I have no manager, and I am free to insist that the prices be kept low so the poor who long for my songs may come and hear them. The color line disappears: rich and poor, high and low, forget the lines that ordinarily divide them, and we all become sons and daughters of a common Father, hushed and quieted by the haunting power of the message of melody and rhythm and song."

Then he told us a story typical, he said, of what was happening to him constantly. In a New Jersey town, a Southern family decided to attend one of his concerts in order to show the fifteen-year-old son "what a horrible mess a nigger makes out of life when he thinks he possesses talents that should be possessed only by white people." The parents had filled the lad with their prejudices ever since he had been able to talk. Mr. Hayes used his usual technique. He blotted himself out of the picture. The rhythm and beauty of God shone through. The atmosphere, now of harmony and peace and now of pathos and sadness, was not marred by the ego of the artist. After the concert, this young man sought out his black brother and threw his arms about his neck. Through his tears he confessed that Mr. Hayes had done in two hours what all the books and orators in the world never could have accomplished. His lifelong prejudice was gone. "And now every time I see him," said Mr. Hayes, "he assures me that he is devoting his life to eradicating prejudice in others similar to what his parents had fostered in him through the years.

"If I thought I could relate it without breaking down, I would tell you about the most remarkable thing that ever happened in my life," Mr. Hayes went on. He finally did relate it, and what a story it was!

"A few years ago, I gave a concert before a large and enthusiastic audience down in Alabama. The next day I journeyed to the old plantation not many miles away where my mother had been a slave. The old master and his wife were still alive, but what a change the years had wrought! The affluence of the old days was gone. The plantation itself had gone to ruin and had been sold for debt. The old gentleman and his wife, upwards of ninety, were existing in a little shanty. I introduced myself and asked them if they remembered my mother. Yes, of course they did—very well indeed. She was one of the dear souls they could never forget. They had called her Pony. Pony was not allowed to live in the slave quarters. She was too much beloved. She would have died for her masters. So, she lived in the big house as a servant."

Mr. Hayes said that as he looked round about at the signs of poverty he could tell the train of thought in the old man's mind—the contrast between the good old days when Pony had been a slave and they had been wealthy, and their present poverty with Pony's son, one of the world's most famous artists, standing before them. He wanted desperately to help them, but wondered whether their Southern pride would permit it.

"So Pony's son has sung before the crowned heads of Europe," mused the old man. "Tell me what you sang for the King and Queen of England."

"I sang a Negro spiritual entitled 'The Crucifixion.'"

"Why, that is the very song your grandfather sang the day he entered the ministry!" exclaimed the old man.

That was a story within a story. The grandfather, converted in Africa through the labors of a missionary, had brought his Christian faith with him when he was sold into slavery in this country and had done some preaching among his brethren. One text had made a very deep impression upon him: "Call no man master, for one is your master, even Christ." He was a hard worker and eventually rose to the position of manager. He could accept bondage, but he could call no man "master." This seemed to the proud owner to be stubbornness, and one day in a fit of anger he killed him.

Knowing that mention of "The Crucifixion" had revived this ancient memory, Mr. Hayes wondered whether this proud old couple would accept his help. He used the familiar spiritual technique of the concert stage and obliterated himself, asking finally if there was anything that Pony's son could do to help. "Yes, I suppose so," came the answer.

"I reached into my pocket and pulled out a check," said Mr. Hayes. "It was a large one—the returns from several of my largest concerts. The old lady was ill and was lying on the bed. I walked over and laid it on her chest. She picked it up and saw the size of it and suddenly realized that it meant getting the old plantation back and ending their days in peace. She screamed and threw open her arms, into which the aged master and I both fell. In a moment we had our arms around each other and were crying like little babies—just three of God's children with no dividing color line. The next day the old man walked five miles, hobbling along on his cane, to hear me sing 'The Crucifixion.' He sat on the front seat and let the tears course unhindered down his wrinkled cheeks."

As we rose to go, I knew that this hour had been the most shining and radiant of my life because of this man's divine consciousness. We were too deeply moved to speak. In the silence and through our tears we merely gripped his hand. After a moment, he asked, "And would you like me to sing 'The Crucifixion' tonight?" The people of Duluth will never forget it—the quiet announcement that two friends had requested it, and the spiritual power that surged through this little black man's soul, sweeping all before it. And as he sang and I recalled the thrilling story of what had happened on that Southern plantation I saw anew, as in a flash of insight, the deeper meaning of the crucifixion itself and of the love that has emanated from it to save and heal and bless mankind.

And now, having told our story, let us ask some searching questions. How did it happen that at the bottom of the depression, when people had little ready cash, Roland Hayes was pulling capacity houses; that even in Southern communities the vexatious color line was disappearing as if by magic; that one of the greatest living artists could be denied the use of the public dining room of his hotel and yet not be hurt by resentment?

The answer is simply that this man knew how to pray! He emptied himself of himself and thus became a clear channel for the Divine. Every breath he drew and every moment of the day was a time of communion with the Eternal Presence. "He that loseth his life for my sake shall find it." Here was no striving after big audiences and glaring publicity; these things just came. "Not by might, nor by power, but by my spirit, saith the Lord." When a man and God walk thus together through all the experiences of each day; when the man thus makes a complete *transfer* of all of his problems and burdens to the strong, sure shoulders of his senior Partner, worry, resentment, and fear can find no resting place. They just are not there. And this, dear friends, is the Secret of Personal Power! This is why the meek, or humble-minded, shall inherit the earth!

Some years ago Charles V. Webber heard a great missionary preach on the kingdom of God, ending with an invitation to any who would like to enter this wonderful kingdom to come to the front. About two thousand people crowded forward, filling the aisle and all available space. The missionary told them to say over and over to themselves as they were dropping off to sleep that night: "I can do all things through Christ which strengtheneth me" (Phil. 4:13). The next morning they were to repeat this Pauline affirmation over and over again. All through day after day for a week, at work or at play, they were slowly and meaningfully to repeat it. Then they were to take other affirmations and start all over again. Thus they would find themselves entering the kingdom of God.

Webber decided that, although he was already a minister, he would give it a try. Before he opened his mail, he would say: "I don't know what is in these letters, but 'I can do all things through Christ which strengtheneth me.' " When his secretary announced a caller, he took a moment alone to repeat his scripture. All day long for a week he kept it up.

Before the week was up, Webber noticed two things. A new sense of joy was bubbling over in his life, and he had a greater flow of physical energy. He could go clear through a grüeling day in high gear.

During the weeks that followed, he took other scriptural affirmations and, by constant repetition, caused them to sink deep into his unconscious mind: "In all thy ways acknowledge him, and he shall direct thy paths" (Prov. 3:6). He came to feel that God was really guiding his life. "Thou wilt keep him in perfect peace, whose mind is stayed on thee" (Isa. 26:3). Using this, he experienced a new and greater peace. One week he tried: "They that wait upon the Lord shall renew their strength; they shall mount up with wings as eagles; they shall run, and not be weary; and they shall walk, and not faint" (Isa. 40:31). And it was true for him. Another week he lived with this one: "My God shall supply all your need according to his riches in glory" (Phil. 4:19).

As we become the living possessors of these eternal truths, we know that the Eternal Presence is with us. They become sources of spiritual and physical energy and power. There is an emanation of spirit that is radiant and friendly in spite of opposition. It leaves no room in our hearts for hatred, and, in Paul's words, we "overcome evil with good."

Silent Communion for Finding the Secret of Power

"He that loseth his life for my sake shall find it" (Matt. 10:39).

"Not by might, nor by power, but by my spirit, saith the Lord" (Zech. 4:6).

"Fear thou not; for I am with thee: be not dismayed; for I am thy God: I will strengthen thee; . . . yea, I will uphold thee with the right hand of my righteousness" (Isa. 41:10).

O my Father, obliterate from my life all self-seeking, all false pride, all conscious or unconscious scheming after first place as thy radiant, healing light and wholeness is channeled through me to bring peace and harmony to the troubled lives of men.

CHAPTER FOURTEEN

The Law of Measures

"Give, and it shall be given unto you; good measure, pressed down, and shaken together, and running over, shall men give into your bosom. *For with the same measure that ye mete withal it shall be measured to you again.*" (Luke 6:38.) Here is Jesus's universal law of measures. Simply put, he is saying: "*In the long run you get out of this universe what you put in*; put in huge amounts of self, time, and substance, and that is what you get back in full, heaped-up measure; put in a little, and back comes a little or maybe nothing at all." In the parable of the talents, the servants to whom ten, five, and two talents were given invested the whole amount and got it back with big interest; but the man who received one talent hoarded instead of investing it, and even that was taken away. He put nothing in; got nothing back.

"Judge not, that ye be not judged. For with what judgment ye judge, ye shall be judged: and with what measure ye mete, it shall be measured to you again." (Matt. 7:1–2.) Are you harsh and unmerciful in your estimates of men? Look out, brother! The cosmic law of measures will take care of you, and you will howl for the mercy which men will refuse to give. "And why beholdest thou the mote [speck] that is in thy brother's eye, but considerest not the beam that is in thine own eye? . . . Thou hypocrite, first cast out the beam out of thine own eye; and then shalt thou see clearly to cast out the mote out of thy brother's eye." (Matt. 7:3, 5.)

This section of the Sermon on the Mount rates a place at the very top of all the utterances ever made concerning the basic law of human relations. It tells us more about the nature of man and the meaning of life, and the importance of conduct than can be found anywhere else in the world. It instructs us more minutely in the art of living and in the secret of happiness and success in the workaday world than do all the writings of the philosophers of the world lumped together from the beginning of time.

Do you doubt this? If so, bring on your most vexing and seemingly insoluble problems in international relations, economics, philosophy, sociology, or religion; bring on any perplexing question in human relations, and examine it with an open mind against Jesus's basic and cosmic Law of Measures, and see where you come out. Tied in closely with this law is the Great Commandment: *Love* God with all your heart, mind, soul, and strength, and your neighbor as yourself. This furnishes the motivation that makes generous giving and generous judging possible. And tied in with the Great Commandment is the law of service, the law which tells us *how* we are to love God and man: "Whosoever will be great among you, let him be your minister; *and whoso-*

ever will be chief among you, let him be your servant: even as the Son of man came not to be ministered unto, but to minister" (Matt. 20:26–28). And there we are right back to Jesus's cosmic Law of Measures. The more we give, the greater we are, and the more we get back. This law is absolute and irrevocable. No one can break it or beat it. All anyone can do is illustrate it. It is like the law of gravitation; jump off the top of the Empire State Building, and your friends, quietly viewing the remains down below, would have to say: "He didn't break the law of gravitation, but he surely illustrated it well!"

Set the question of gambling over against the Law of Measures. A man places a two-dollar bet against a certain horse and wins one hundred dollars. He is elated; he has made ninety-eight dollars by just guessing right! He says: "What a lucky bum I am!" "Bum" is right, because see what probably follows. He gets into the gambling game now in a big way. Maybe he makes more quick profits. Life is wonderful. After a while, if he remains lucky (?), he quits his regular job and becomes a professional gambler. He then associates with men who work shady practices like bribing a basketball player or doping a horse or buying an officer of the law. Then a weak link in the chain gives way, the big exposé is on, and our friend goes to the penitentiary or is felled by a gangster's bullet. Too late, he ruefully admits: "You can't, in the long run, get something for nothing out of a universe that is governed by the Law of Measures. *Put nothing in and you get nothing out*— and even the little you had will be taken away!"

On the international scene, just read a little history and note the fallen empires which followed the gangster technique. Forget the Assyrian, Babylonian, Egyptian, and Roman empires which illustrated this law in the long ago and come on down to modern times. In 1934, Jan Smuts the former Boer general and Prime Minister of South Africa, gave an address on freedom at Scotland's St. Andrews University. Looking at Hitler, Mussolini, and Stalin, all then in full strut and riding high, he said that people might well be gloomy if they thought only of the moment. Freedom was weaker in Europe than for centuries past; tyranny had overspread most of the continent. "But," said Smuts, "freedom is the most ineradicable craving of human nature. The denial of free human rights must in the long run lead to a cataclysm." He was right; within a few years, the dictatorships of Hitler and Mussolini were as extinct as those of twenty-one others that Toynbee says have walked the road to dusty death for violating the Law of Measures.

And Stalin? He is dead, and there is every indication of serious trouble behind the Iron Curtain. Give those new leaders time, and see what happens! A nation that claims to be changing the world for the better while grabbing nation after nation and sucking them dry, a nation that scoffs at all religious and ethical values while enslaving millions and denying them even the rudiments of the good life, a nation that belongs to the United Nations only in order the better to sabotage all efforts at international understanding and world peace is doomed. Have patience. Give them time. Our cosmic Law of Measures will again be demonstrated.

To come closer to home, how much are you getting out of your church? How much are you putting into it? The answer to the latter question is the real answer to the former. Someone has said that there are two classes of people in every church—those who do all the work and those who are perfectly willing that they should! The workers have all the joy of accomplishment, while the shirkers make all the excuses for their nonparticipation. The workers pour in their money, time, and talents until the shirkers often wonder why they do. Well, ask them. Or better still, ask the author of the Sermon on the Mount. "*For with the same measure you use, it shall be measured to you again.*"

The other day, a lady in California sent me a newspaper story of a minister who had become weary of listening to the many excuses of people who go to the movies a lot but seldom go to church. So, in delightful, satirical vein, he gave his people ten reasons why he seldom attended the movies:

1. The manager of the theater never called on me.
2. I did go a few times, but no one spoke to me. Those who go there aren't very friendly.
3. Every time I go they ask me for money.
4. Not all folks live up to the high moral standards of the films.
5. I went so much as a child, I've had all the entertainment I need.
6. The performance lasts too long. I can't sit still for an hour and three-quarters.

7. I don't care for some of the people I see and meet at the theater.
8. I don't always agree with what I hear and see.
9. I don't think they have very good music at the theater.
10. The shows are held in the evenings, and that's the only time I am able to be at home with the family.

No, dear friends, do not waste any pity on the people who carry the load in church, Sunday school, P.T.A., Red Cross, lodge, United World Federalists, or any other group dedicated to community betterment. "By their fruits ye shall know them." When the Judge in heaven shall finally say: "Come, ye blessed of my Father, inherit the kingdom prepared for you from the foundation of the world," he will be talking to them. These are they who will have had such a good time giving generously of their time, sympathy, and energy that they will be surprised at their good fortune. "Lord, when saw we thee an hungred, and fed thee? or thirsty, and gave thee drink? When saw we thee a stranger, and took thee in? or naked, and clothed thee? Or when saw we thee sick, or in prison, and came unto thee? And the King shall answer and say unto them, Verily I say unto you, Inasmuch as ye have done it unto one of the least of these my brethren, ye have done it unto me." (Matt. 25:37–40.) *This Law of Measures spans two worlds!*

A word of caution needs to be injected just here, however. Indiscriminate giving may well ruin the recipient. The needy must be helped only with wisdom and good judgment. Otherwise, we may make ungrateful chiselers and liars out of them; and we may aid and abet them in their indolence and thus cause them to break our Law of Measures.

Jacob Panken is one of eighteen justices of Domestic Relations Court in New York City which deals with the city's household disasters—cases of nonsupport, abandonment, and juvenile delinquency. Most of the twenty thousand cases that have come before Judge Panken's court originate with families on relief. Here is a family of the type that worries the Judge. The father had not worked for fifteen months because he said he was not well. A doctor said there was nothing wrong with him except too much alcohol bought with relief money. A strapping eighteen-year-old son, favorite child of the father, did not work or go to school either, and he had plenty of pocket money supplied by the father. Three younger children were half starved and in rags, and they said their mother gave them little time or attention. This family had been receiving $3,180 a year from the welfare fund and spending much of it on drink while turning down good jobs because of "ill health." Such giving is immoral because it ruins character. Judge Panken ordered the father to go to work.

Then there was a family of thirteen, all public charges in New York City. Seven of the children were in foster homes at a cost of $110 a week. The father, instead of looking for a job, went fishing every day. Or, there was the Nelson family (not a real name). They had been on relief for fifteen years, during which time ten children were born at the expense of the city. The children had become delinquents. They did not attend a free public school regularly. According to the Judge that one family had cost the state $35,000, and the end was not yet!

The whole family welfare problem of New York City needs overhauling if more thousands are not to be ruined. Nearly 5 per cent of the city's population—387,000 individuals—are on relief. And these are prosperous times indeed. Here is the Law of Measures in reverse. To receive without giving anything in return is highly immoral. In such a case, the giver is more at fault than the receiver, because he is in a position to remedy the situation if he will.

The depth of Jesus's insight into human nature is well illustrated by his Law of Measures. Give constructively of your time, talents and substance, and the universe will give it back with interest. Why then do so many children use this law in reverse and do wrong things that result in a terrific problem of juvenile delinquency? The answer is that adults have not been giving enough of their own creative thought and energy to the children. Parents, teachers, ministers, and officers of the law should know that children are not born good or bad but do come into the world with tremendous *capacities* for goodness or badness. They are little "muscle people" with great driving energy that must be properly channeled into constructive projects if it is not to find its way into destructive outlets.

The Washington *Post* of November 11, 1951, carried the story "Badges Keep Boys Out of Mischief." It all started some years ago when the National Sheriffs' Association, meeting in Washington, had the wisdom to form the Junior Deputy Sheriffs' League. More than a million boys in more than five hundred counties of all forty-eight states belong. They range in age from seven to seventeen years. The basic idea is very simple: A county sheriff calls in all available boys of those ages and tells them he needs help in tracking down lawbreakers and in making a good law-abiding community. He shows them a bright Junior Deputy Sheriff's badge and tells them that the old game of cops and robbers is kid stuff but this is the real thing. He will pin a badge on any kid, he says, if that youngster wants to help keep the county clean and law-abiding. Experience shows that they join up en masse.

"What's happened in Logan County?" asked Jessie Riley, superintendent of the West Virginia Boys' Reform School, in a note to Judge C. C. Chambers of the juvenile court in Logan. "We're not getting any more boys from there."

The Junior Deputy Sheriffs' League is the answer there as it has been in hundreds of communities across the nation. Six-sevenths of Logan County's 80,000 people are dependent on the mines. Dingy gray houses line the mountain sides in row upon row. Because there are no decent yards or playgrounds, fighting and thieving and destroying were about all a live, energetic boy could find to do. Grover Combs, when he became sheriff, sent out a call to all the juveniles of the county to come and see him on September 1, 1949. What was his surprise and joy to count 2,368 boys from twelve to seventeen years of age lined up on the courthouse lawn. He had ordered only 500 badges, but he promised more within a few days. All signed up, and Logan County had a whole army of youngsters out looking for anybody who dared to start trouble.

One young deputy saw a woman's purse lying on the counter in a dime store. When nobody came to claim it, he opened it and found $24.18 but no name. So he took it to Sheriff Combs, who said it was the first purse with money in it that had ever been turned in to him. Halloween had always been a nightmare of destruction in Logan County, but October 31 of 1949 passed without a single misdemeanor being reported!

The movement very wisely has gone much further than that, however. You can't spend all your time looking for lawbreakers—not if you are a live boy. So, $15,000 a year was appropriated in that county for recreational equipment and for the hiring of two trained leaders to keep the boys busy and happy.

Paul C. Winter, superintendent of the Logan County school district, reports that truancy has all but disappeared and vandalism has reached the vanishing point. It used to cost $5,000 a year to repair school property damaged during the summer. The only damage done in the summer of 1951 was to one school where there were no Junior Deputies. In 1952 there was not a single case of juvenile delinquency in the county!

This remarkable record is being duplicated in nearly a sixth of the nation's 3,069 counties. They do not have to preach to the boys or threaten them or beg them to be good. They just give them real jobs on the side of law and order, and the boys get such joy out of doing constructive work that the problem of delinquency evaporates. Just imagine three small boys in Arizona, reading Sheriff John Peery Francis's bulletin which describes a tall, redheaded woman who has passed $50.00 worth of bad checks in Flagstaff. Our young sleuths go out on the prowl. Passing a graveyard, they see a tall, redheaded woman strolling among the tombs. One boy streaks it for the sheriff's office, while the other two hide and watch. Out comes Sheriff Francis, and sure enough—she is the wanted culprit! Proud? Those boys will never be the same again. They are for law and order!

"Judge not . . . for with what judgment ye judge, ye shall be judged." Dr. Howard Thurman, while he was living in our home and teaching in the School of Religion at the University of Iowa, told a story about his remarkable mother-in-law, Mrs. S. E. Bailey, of Arkansas. She was greatly troubled over the racial prejudice of the county sheriff, who hated all Negroes and had as a motto: "When you catch a nigger in trouble shoot him first, and ask questions later." When he became ill and was lying at the point of death in the hospital, Mrs. Bailey gathered a whole washtub full of beautiful flowers from among her colored friends and sent them to the sheriff with this note: "From your many Negro friends who are praying for your recovery." He looked at them a long while and then said: "I didn't know I had any friends among the Negroes; but if I ever get well I'll be a friend to them all." He did—and he was.

Silent Communion for Obeying the Law of Measures

"You must be merciful, just as your Father is. Do not judge others, and they will not judge you. Do not condemn them, and they will not condemn you. Excuse others and they will excuse you. Give, and they will give to you: good measure, pressed down, shaken together, and running over, they will pour into your lap. For the measure you use with others they in turn will use with you." (Luke 6:36–38, Goodspeed translation.)

I am judging all men in mercy, love, and understanding. I am engaged continuously in a blessed outgoingness without thought of personal return. I am giving the best that is in me to friends, acquaintances, and enemies alike—and with God's Law of Measures be the rest!

CHAPTER FIFTEEN

Health and Restful Sleep

Three years ago, I was giving a series of Lenten talks at Trinity Methodist Church in Kansas City. One evening I spoke briefly of the art of sleeping well and remarked that perhaps in the next talk I would give poor sleepers some simple directions for overcoming insomnia.

The next evening a very large audience put me into a happy frame of mind, and I got so interested in what I was saying that I forgot all about my promise. I finally dismissed them, and was mystified when not a soul moved. They just sat there looking at me! Finally a lady arose and said: "A great many of us came here tonight expecting you to tell us how to cure insomnia, and we haven't heard a word about it." When they were reminded that another half-hour would be needed for going into that baffling subject, they gave smiling and unanimous consent. Thereupon I said some of the things I will repeat now, including a simple formula for putting one's self to sleep soon after going to bed or for causing the return of sleep if one awakens in the middle of the night.

Afterward, a young woman about thirty years of age came to the chancel and said: "Sounds very plausible, but I know it won't work. I've tried everything, and I haven't had a sound night's sleep in five years." I then outlined again the simple procedure which will presently be given here and challenged her to try it that very night with confidence, and to report the results. The next evening she came up with an apologetic grin and said: "Do you know, it worked! I slept all night for the first time I can remember." Nor is she the only insomnia victim who has had a similar experience.

When Macbeth in Shakespeare's play laments his loss of "sleep that knits up the ravell'd sleave of care, . . . balm of hurt minds," he describes its function well. In sleep, not disturbed by the frettings of consciousness, we touch a source of magic renewal and refreshment found nowhere else. In natural sleep the dark forebodings of the midnight hours disappear, the waste products that have accumulated through the long, tedious hours of the waking day are carried off as new strength and vitality come surging in. During a good night of sound sleep, the cares that have infested the day fold their tents like the Arabs, and as silently steal away.

That is the way a child sleeps. He needs to learn to walk, but he does not need to learn how to sleep. As the shadows lengthen and the day draws near its close, the Sandman comes seeking the child and finds him. Look at him there in his crib dead to the world! He doesn't know it, but many a millionaire would give his fortune to be able to sleep like that again. Recently one of my sons moved into a new house in Maywood, Illinois. Little Buzzie, aged two, ran for hours with joyous abandon all over the house and yard. Presently the parents missed him and, a bit frightened, began searching everywhere. They found him, curled up in a corner of the couch, asleep. The little guy doesn't know how blessed he is!

One of the causes of wakefulness is our sedentary way of living. We do not exercise enough in the fresh air. At the University of Iowa about half of the students own cars and drive from class to class, when a brisk walk would help to sweep the cobwebs out of the mind. One of Jimmy Hatlo's "They'll Do It Every Time" cartoons drives home this point. The first part of the cartoon shows Dimbulb buying a new home one block from the suburban station. "It will be good for me to walk to the train every morning," he smilingly confides to the real estate agent. The second picture shows Dimbulb dashing out of the back door with a cup of coffee in his hand and coat tails flying as the little woman backs the car out of the garage at 7:59 and the train whistles for the station. "Step on it, what are you waiting for," he cries. Below, Hatlo comments: "Six months, and he hasn't walked yet!" What an hour's brisk walk every day would do for the average able-bodied man or woman when the lights are out and it's time to sleep!

Improper diet is another cause of sleeplessness. Our bodies

are fearfully and wonderfully made. They contain the same elements as any good acre of land. However, when the rich topsoil is mined away by taking from it crop after crop without any renewals, and it is exposed to erosion, certain elements disappear. Crops grown on such land cannot absorb elements that are no longer there. The result is devitalized food. The human body in turn is deprived of what it needs, and maladjustment is sure to follow.

We all comprehend why an automobile deprived of good oil wears and rattles and finally breaks down. It is just so with the body when basic elements are lacking in our food. Down in the Tennessee valley a quarter of a century ago, the people in general were scrawny, ill nourished, sickly, and cantankerous because they were eating food grown on ruined land. Came then the great T.V.A. that rebuilt the washed-out soil. Today, one finds a revitalized people because they are eating the kind of food their bodies must have to function properly. On an inspection tour of the valley sometime ago, I heard from numbers of these fine people that they were sleeping better, eating better, and enjoying life as never before.

Too much rich food is just as bad as too little, especially when eaten late at night. Millions of people will go to a party, smoke and drink all evening, and then fill their stomachs with rich, rare foods about midnight. No wonder they cannot sleep well. Doctors tell us that, generally speaking, no food should pass our lips after an ample evening meal. The stomach should be empty when we retire; otherwise, that chemical factory has to work all night converting food just taken into an assimilable form of energy.

The greatest sleep robbers of all, however, are the worries, fear and guilt complexes that we have carried around all day and think about after we have retired. The last things we think about before dropping off to sleep are the things which remain closest to the surface of the unconscious mind and are apt to spring first into consciousness when we awaken in the night. Then, if we have no technique for putting ourselves back to sleep, if we have no definite system of thought control, these worries start churning round and round like a squirrel in a revolving cage, and we are in for several miserable hours of wakefulness. Add to that the fear that we shall soon have to get up and face the new day more tired than when we went to bed, and we are really in for it! The "ravell'd sleave of care" ravels still further until we feel like a ragbag rather than a rested and vital human being.

Sleeping pills are definitely not the answer to insomnia except under extraordinary circumstances and under doctor's orders. If they are taken regularly, the dosage must be increased. These larger amounts of drugs have a toxic effect and make the next day a nightmare of listlessness. Physicians now tell us that sleeping pills taken regularly over a long period of time tend to destroy the nerve centers.

Sound sleep is largely a matter of thought control. The power of suggestion must be properly comprehended and utilized in the most positive way. This is the key to relaxation, without which refreshing sleep is impossible. Elwood Worcester, famous rector of Emmanuel Church in Boston, was also a psychiatrist. Through his clinic over a period of twenty-five years there passed many thousands of troubled souls. He taught them how to confess their sins and worries and fears, how to relax, how to trust God, how to sleep. He said that when he finally left Emmanuel Church, the only object he asked permission to take with him was an old Morris chair in which he had treated thousands of men, women, and children.

Again and again Dr. Worcester said to patients stretched out in that old Morris chair:

" 'I wish you would let your thought travel slowly downward over the parts of your body. All the way down your back the muscles and joints are relaxing and your back is flattening against the chair, your waist, your hips, your knees, your ankles and your feet. Your jaws are loosely closed, you are not clenching your teeth. As your body becomes so still and quiet, your mind is passing into the same condition. Your thoughts are less vivid. They are becoming vague and dim and uncertain. You do not think of anything distinctly. You can let yourself go down into rest and peace, down, down, down, down, deeper, deeper, deeper, deeper. As you are not using your brain actively, the blood tends to recede from your head and pass into your body and into your limbs. Your forehead is cool: your arms and legs are heavy and relaxed, as if it would be an effort to move them; and you wish to make no effort. As your other muscles relax, your eyelids do.'

"Then, if I felt the patient had not fully responded, I might paint a few dissolving pictures of the coming of the night beside some lovely lake, or of gliding down some clear, wilderness river in a canoe, after the manner of the spirits' song as they lulled Faust to sleep." *

Dr. Worcester tells us that he does not attempt to put the patient entirely to sleep by this method: "I usually explain to my patients that if their conscious, active thought is in abeyance, I can address my suggestions more readily to the subconscious mind *which controls both our moods and our physical processes and which is subject to suggestion.*" † Remember that when an affirmation is repeated again and again, either by one's self or by a counselor, the deep mind must accept it and bring it into manifestation. That is the law of mind. The Creator made us that way. Prayer, faith, and suggestion are tied together with an indissoluble bond. Our great care must always be to keep our critical conscious mind on the job sifting truth from falsehood so that we allow ourselves to dwell only on what is true. God will then bring that to fruition through faith, suggestion, and affirmation.

Now, having established the function and place and

* Elwood Worcester and Samuel McComb, *Body, Mind and Spirit* (Boston, 1931), p. 196. Courtesy Charles Scribner's Sons, New York, who now hold the rights.

† *Ibid.*, p. 197.

power of suggestion in any workable technique for putting ourselves to sleep, let us list a number of successive steps that, if taken in this order, will positively accomplish the desired results.

1. Think only pleasant thoughts for at least an hour befor retiring. Please do not tell me you cannot help yourself at this point; that if you are worried you are worried and cannot keep out such thoughts. When a woman from another city sat in my counseling chair sometime ago and said that to me I spoke very sharply: "What are you? A weak namby-pamby soul who has no control whatsoever over her trains of thought, who must sit helplessly by while fear and worry thoughts take over the citadel of her consciousness? What you need is some *iron in your blood*! Say to yourself, '*I* am in control here, and I now decree that before I go to sleep I shall concentrate only on the God of love, peace, poise, power, and radiance. No negative thought shall be allowed to come in, for there will be no room!' When a room is full of light, darkness just is not there. Get into the driver's seat, and stay there. Assert dominion, and demonstrate your power of control." Later, this woman sent a letter of gratitude and a check for my radio program. She wrote: "It works, and how much better I feel already!" Of course it works! And it can work for you, too, my reader friend!

2. When you get into bed, settle yourself in the most comfortable and restful position and use the power of suggestion to relax along lines used by Dr. Worcester. Put the

smile of confidence on your face. You will be surprised to discover how tense your face was; then go on down the entire body. Unbend! Relax! Let go!

3. Repeat an old promise from the Bible: "He giveth his beloved sleep." Say it slowly a dozen times, and believe it. Also: "Underneath are the everlasting arms." Cradle yourself thus in the arms of the Infinite. Give yourself this great basic security, this blessed safety: "I will both lay me down in peace, and sleep: for thou, Lord, only, makest me dwell in safety." Learn these promises by heart so that there is no effort at remembering them. Repeat them over and over, slowly, meaningfully, until the deep mind can do nothing else than bring them into glorious, sleep-productng manifestation.

4. *Visualize yourself as sound asleep.* If your flitting mind begins to wander, assert your mastery and dominion and bring it back to the business in hand—but do not worry about it. Smile, and keep concentrating on the vision and the verses.

5. *Let your breathing be deep, very deep, regular, and rhythmical.* This is important. The body and mind love rhythm. The blood stream is thereby purified by an abundance of fresh air (we assume you have a window open!), and this soothes your tired nerves. If your wayward mind sneaks back to a worry thought, you will find that you have stopped breathing deeply and are hardly breathing at all. Smile at this low-down double cross, and get right back on the beam.

Well, that's all there is to it. If you do these five things and keep on doing them, you are bound to sleep. If you awaken in the night, put yourself back to sleep by the same technique before the fear-worry train of thought has a chance to get you wide awake.

On a summer vacation a woman told me she had not had one good night's sleep for years. Her husband had died, leaving her with a large family to support. Two breast cancers had been removed, and the operations had shattered her nerves and her confidence. I told her of the above technique and guaranteed she could not help sleeping if she did exactly as I suggested. She had "tried everything," but promised to give it a good try. The next morning she looked quite refreshed. "Doggone it!" she said. "I hate to admit that you were right, but it worked."

And here is one for the record. When I was working on this chapter last night, the very writing out of those affirmations made me so sleepy that I had to go to bed! I arose at six this morning to finish it and almost went to sleep again!

Silent Communion for Restful Sleep

"He giveth his beloved sleep" (Psalm 127:2).

"I will both lay me down in peace, and sleep: for thou, Lord, only, makest me dwell in safety" (Psalm 4:8).

"Come unto me, all ye that labour and are heavy laden, and I will give you *rest*" (Matt. 11:28).

Down, down, down, down I glide, cradled in the everlasting arms of the Infinite Love and Eternal Rest.

CHAPTER SIXTEEN

A Channel for Healing Power

Living quietly in the city of Minneapolis before her recent death was an elderly lady who had been a channel for the flow of healing power for more than forty years. Margueritte Harmon Bro has recently given us the life story of Mrs. Harrie Vernette Rhodes. Through the years this modest little woman had been laying her frail hands on the diseased bodies of people; and, in many cases, she had brought them healing of body and soul. Furthermore, she seems to have been guided in her work by some of God's busy angels. She tried to follow their directions with scrupulous care, and many of the results would appear to be most remarkable.

After reading *In the One Spirit*, I discussed it with Dr. Marcus Bach of the School of Religion at the State University of Iowa. He has long taught a course on "Little Known Religions," and together we have often journeyed to investigate some religious phenomena. At his suggestion I telephoned to Mrs. Rhodes, and two weeks later we were on the night train for Minneapolis. There were two days each week when she could see curious visitors—Monday and

Thursday. These two days she reserved for rest, meditation, and prayer. All other days were booked solid from seven-thirty in the morning long into the night. She showed us her date book, and it was black with names at twenty-minute intervals for several days ahead. She had never commercialized her healing gift and made no charge for her services. If anyone wished to leave a gift, as most visitors did, it was gratefully received, because she had no other source of income. Many, however, were too destitute to do very much.

The taximan who took us to her home seemed to be familiar with her work. He volunteered the opinion that, if he should be taken ill, he would make a bee line to the "healing lady." Asked if he brought many people there, he replied that he did. "Only yesterday I took a very happy man out there," he said. "When I took him there for the first time, you should have seen him—on crutches and all crippled up with arthritis, groaning with pain every time I hit a bump in the road. Yesterday, one month later, the man had no crutches, and he was as spry as a cricket—you should have heard him sing the little lady's praises."

Although Mrs. Rhodes was past eighty and followed a daily schedule that would tax the vitality of one forty years her junior, she gave the entire day to telling us about her work and answering our questions. She did not look strong, but gave sure evidence of remarkable vitality. She was self-effacing and modest, making no claims other than that she had been used by invisible and heavenly powers as a channel for healing. Why she had been chosen, she did not know.

She would simply put one frail hand at the back of the ailing person's neck and the other one on his solar plexus and pray. Healing power flowed through.

Dr. Bach and I must have looked puzzled at this simple explanation, for she smiled and said, "Lie down on the couch on your back and relax, and I'll give you a demonstration." I lay down first. She moved a low stool up beside me, sat down and placed her hands in the required position. I remarked that it was a pity, under the circumstances, that I did not have an ache or a pain. Nevertheless, I could distinctly feel a current of power flowing through her hands. I was a bit weary from the train ride, but in ten minutes I felt relaxed and rested and at peace with the world. Dr. Bach had the same experience.

The realization of her power to transmit healing came to Mrs. Rhodes quite by accident more than forty years ago. A neighbor, Mrs. Wenzel, had been an invalid for five years, having had five operations, and suffering great pain from an acute form of arthritis. One afternoon Mrs. Rhodes made a friendly call and found her ready to move from her big chair into her bed but dreading the pain that was sure to accompany the effort. To help her, Mrs. Rhodes told us, "I put my hands on her, one beneath her shoulders, the other on her chest. We both felt the quickening sensation that pulsed between my hands. She said: 'What are you doing? Did you ever do this kind of thing before?' " Mrs. Rhodes left her hands in that position awhile after her neighbor was in bed. Presently she was sound asleep, and the next morning she walked down to breakfast, astounding herself. After a few more treatments she was well; and she stayed that way.

Mrs. Rhodes's father died in 1902, and some years later he began coming to her in various ways. Sometimes she would sit in a darkened room with pencil and paper and receive messages from him. On January 17, 1910, this is what she found on the paper: "The thoughts in your heart make so much difference. If you think loving thoughts, full of cheer and success, we can so much more easily help you to get those things. If you are blue or unloving, you cannot draw to yourself the best things in life. Do not allow your doubts or fears to make an atmosphere about you. Know that God is love and you are His forever. Rest more, rest every way. Drop out fear, worry, sorrow; rest in peace and love."

She was sure that it was her father speaking to her, because she sometimes heard him speaking in the voice that was so familiar. At other times she actually saw him. This happened first in June, 1911: "I awoke to see my father standing by my bedside. I mean just that; he looked like himself, dressed as he used to dress. Since then he has often appeared to me. Usually his figure is not at all transparent, and yet I would say that it has no weight except that when he is talking to me, I am not dwelling on his looks, actually, but upon his presence and what he is imparting. Sometimes I only half visualize him; his form is indistinct but his presence is real. At other times I do not see him at all, but I hear his voice plainly; I hear him laugh." *

* *In the One Spirit*, autobiography of Harrie Vernette Rhodes as told to Marguerite Harmon Bro (New York: Harper & Brothers, 1951), pp. 56–57.

On this particular occasion, her father told her that her new work of healing was about to commence in earnest, and that she would need a new and more accessible residence. He directed her to a location on Nicollet Avenue in Minneapolis which, she found, fitted the description as he had given. She moved in, and thus began the work that has gone on to the present day.

Before leaving the subject of John Henry Rhodes and his signed messages to his daughter through automatic writing, I beg leave to quote one remarkable letter in full. It contains the truth about what determines one's status in the future life as I have long considered it to be from a study of the teachings of Jesus. If this truth could really sink into our dull minds, some of our lives might take a different direction:

"It has come to me that if people on the earth plane could see some of the scenes which are common in my work, it would be a great help to them in their daily life. My work is that of a guide. On earth I might be called a missionary, and that term may be more easily understood by some who read this message. My duty is to meet those entrusted to my care as they come from earth life, show them how to live, and see that they are comfortably located and given work whereby they may grow and also help others.

"Perhaps a few cases which I have met will give you a better idea of what this life is like. There are some who have lived on earth a life of formalism, where everything was done in some special religious form, without the spirit back of it. There is really no harder class to help than these persons for they cannot think or understand that the 'letter killeth, but the spirit giveth life.'

"I well remember a lady who had been accustomed to repeating forms of prayers without once thinking of their meaning, and the difficulty I had in rousing her attention enough so she would listen to me. She knew she had passed through some change, but did not know exactly what had happened. If you could have seen her joy when she realized that life is not made of empty words, but of real living deeds, and had you been able to follow her through her work of saving those who had been in the same darkness as herself, you would have learned a lesson you could never forget. The lesson is so seldom taught on earth that one pure desire is more fruitful than a lifetime of mere forms, that many are held back by the belief that a certain number of prayers per day will be all they need. 'Prayer is the soul's sincere desire,' and that is what brings results into a life.

"Another case was of a man who had been considered a bad man because he did not live up to all the rules taught him by his priest. He came here with the thought that of course he must go into a lake of fire, for he had not kept up his church duties. I found him cowering in a dark place, waiting to be borne into hell. I said to him, 'Friend, why are you here in this manner?' After an amazed silence, he told me what had happened and his expectation. I saw in his life much that was good, many kind deeds, and above all, the loving spirit that helped the helpless and those in trouble, expecting no return but the knowledge that some were made happier. When he saw that his old fears were a mistake, that the living love in a life, not the outward forms, is what counts, his joy was wonderful and he is doing all he can to bring this knowledge to others.

"Again, there comes to mind a soul who considered himself far better than most people. He had been an autocrat on earth. When he came here he looked around for his servants and was about to order someone to wait upon him. No one could convince him that he was one of the poorest and most desolate of souls, for his whole life had been one of selfishness and he knew nothing of the joy of living for others. The Christlike spirit of love was a mere name to him, and there he had to stay in a barren spot, waiting for the time when he could have a desire to do something for someone else; for only by doing for others and forgetting self could he grow upward.

"Among others was a woman who had always given her life to help others in distress and had spent little thought on herself. She had known that she was God's child and had trusted Him to take care of her. When she was shown her new home and saw all the beauty and harmony which had been placed there by her loving, beautiful life on earth, she cried, 'Indeed, my soul is satisfied!' There was the music for which her soul had longed, but which she had been too busy to get; there, the beautiful paintings, the harmony of life which no mortal can comprehend, the outgrowth of a sweet life lived on earth.

"Contrast this spirit mansion with the house created by a life of self-seeking, and no one would for a moment wish to exchange the one for the other. How cheerless and barren the home made by selfish thoughts and deeds. Could people see the houses their lives of pleasure-seeking and materialism build, they would at once change their mode of living.

"The statement that your life builds you a home is perhaps new and strange to you, but let me tell you, it is nevertheless, true. All your thoughts and actions are entering into the character which you are building and which will determine what sort of dwelling you will inhabit in your future life. It is only by having the Christ Spirit in your lives that you can build the right kind of houses. He lives in your hearts and by His constant leadership, His tender love and fellowship, He teaches you the lesson of life and love which is embodied in His two great commandments: 'Thou shalt love the Lord thy God with all thy heart and with all thy mind and with all thy strength; and the second is like unto it, thou shalt love thy neighbor as thyself!' Love is the fulfilling of the law. How beautiful your heavenly home will be to you if filled with the love and gratitude of those whom you helped on earth! Far different will it be if made by selfishness and ornamented with an array of unused opportunities, and the sorrows and tears caused by your carelessness and lack of love.

"Let these thoughts of the future life influence your daily life on earth, that you may be transformed into the likeness of Him who came to teach you how to live. 'Let this same spirit be in you which was in Christ Jesus, that you may be transformed by the renewing of your mind,' and in so doing you will be fitted for a life of usefulness and beauty in the life to come, which is but a continuance of your present life. (Signed) John Henry Rhodes." *

In discussing the messages received through automatic writing, Mrs. Rhodes admitted to Dr. Bach and me that trite and meaningless communications often come through to others through the same type of channel because there are plenty of shallow and mischievous souls over there who love to talk when they have little to say; but she was seldom bothered by such people because she was on her guard against them. Her father always signed his messages and always gave her something worth while that had the mark of his own fine insight and character.

After talking through a long morning, Mrs. Rhodes informed us that we were to accompany her to lunch with a friend. A taxi was called, and we crossed the city to a lovely suburban home. Our friendly hostess, Mrs. H. P., served a delicious meal and then told us her story. She was a doctor's wife and had gone through a sea of trouble. I judged that her trouble was psychosomatic; that disappointment and sorrow had caused the physical paralysis that confined her to a bed for five long years. At any rate, she finally heard about Mrs. Rhodes, and that lady, answering her call, placed her hands on the helpless body over a succession of weeks, healing both her soul and her body. Now Mrs. H. P. has been doing her own work for several years.

During the forty-odd years that Mrs. Rhodes practiced

* *Ibid.*, pp. 100–104.

the art of healing, she treated thousands of people who had a great variety of diseases. She believed she benefited most of them, if not all. It is a pity that we do not have a good doctor's diagnosis on some of them; but such records, quite understandably, are not available. It is estimated that well over half of all the ills of humanity are mentally induced through worry, fear, and feelings of guilt. Such ills are not truly organic but functional. The pain is just as great with a functional disturbance as with one that is truly organic, and, for all practical purposes, the patient is just as ill. Only in recent years have doctors come to recognize the psychosomatic (body and soul) character of many of these ills.

I am not suggesting here that it is impossible for God and his busy angels to cure organic diseases through faith and the laying on of hands. The earlier chapter, "The Guard at the Door," relates the authenticated story of the faith healing of Lieutenant Commander Edwin Miller Rosenberg after he had been given up for lost to the dread disease of cancer. Dr. Leslie D. Weatherhead's monumental work, *Psychology, Religion and Healing*, makes an exhaustive study of this very subject, examining much documentary evidence and exploring many case histories, certified by competent doctors, to show that such healing does happen. However, his book is full of grave warnings against cults and healers who advise people to leave their doctors and rely on faith healing alone to cure their ills. He advises people to work *with* their doctors and ministers and healers. So do I. This combination will frequently effect cures where either alone would fail.

As Dr. Bach and I took the train for home, we tried to evaluate Mrs. Rhodes. We felt that she was a genuine, non-self-seeking channel for the flow of healing power; that she had been the means of healing people's souls as well as their bodies. Why are some people selected to act as channels for the flow of healing power and not others? We do not know. Had she actually received messages from God's busy angels? Undoubtedly she had, as has happened to countless numbers of people from Jesus's day to this. The mere fact that an event does not come within my personal experience is no reason to suppose it did not happen to Mrs. Rhodes and others like her. Our knowledge of the material universe has far outstripped our knowledge of the spiritual side of life. The electrical wizard Steinmetz was undoubtedly correct prophesying that the next fifty years would witness the greatest imaginable progress in our understanding and use of spiritual power, not only for the healing of diseased bodies, but also for the development and growth of harmony and peace in all the affairs of mankind.

Silent Communion for Demonstrating Healing Power

"And he [Jesus] called to him his twelve disciples and gave them authority . . . to heal every disease and every infirmity" (Matt. 10:1, Revised Standard Version).

Healing power has been demonstrated by some of Christ's followers all through the centuries. Jesus's own brother

James commanded: ". . . pray one for another, that ye may be healed" (James 5:16).

I am holding the perfect image of my whole self in the presence of God as his healing power is vitalizing every cell of my body.

CHAPTER SEVENTEEN

Busy Angels

Many of the spiritually great of past centuries have been very certain that they were in frequent contact with heavenly beings. George Fox, St. Francis of Assisi, St. Catherine of Siena, St. Theresa, Jakob Boehme of Silesia, Emanuel Swedenborg, Alfred Russel Wallace, and many others believed that they had "flashes," visions from above, and direct guidance from heavenly beings. George Fox, apostle of the Inner Light, had a divine warning of the great fire of London and also of the outbreak of the Revolution of 1688 before these events took place. Swedenborg sat with friends in William Castel's house in Gothenburg, Sweden, and described a fire at that moment raging in Stockholm, as proved by dispatches two days later. He was "told" of it by people in the land of spirit.

The Bible is full of a belief in angels who have contact with our world. Psalm 91:11 declares: "He shall give his angels charge over thee, to keep thee in all thy ways." When Jesus had been tempted for forty days in the wilderness, "angels came and ministered unto him" (Matt. 4:11). On one occasion he admonished his disciples: "Take heed that ye despise not one of these little ones; for I say unto you, That in heaven *their angels* do always behold the face of my Father which is in heaven" (Matt. 18:10). This is a direct reference to the existence of guardian angels. Jesus, rebuking Peter in the Garden of Gethsemane for cutting off the ear of the high priest's servant, stoutly declared that he could have obtained from his Father "more than twelve legions of angels" if he had wished protection (Matt. 26:53).

The kingdom of God seems to be peopled with angels who are busy helping the Heavenly Father with a thousand and one tasks that need attention. And why not? In this world a good executive is one who knows how to delegate authority to others. That is the way great men are developed—by assuming ever greater and greater responsibility. And why should it not also be true in the next world? If personality values are the only eternal values, and if persons gradually unfold and grow as they successfully grapple with the problems of earthly existence, why should the same plan not be continued after death? Can anyone think of a better way for us to continue to grow "unto a perfect man, unto the measure of the stature of the fulness of Christ"? It seems logical to believe that many of the strange compulsions that cause us to make this choice or that, in spite of worldly evidence that points in another direction, may be caused by God's busy angels.

Here is a remarkable incident that came to me in a letter from Dr. Frederick R. Taylor of High Point, North Carolina, after he had read my book *Something to Stand On*:

"You might be interested in my experience. Insulin had just become available to me in my practice. The first patient I treated was threatened with coma in hospital. Of course, only the original 'quick' insulin of short duration in its effects was available then. The patient was a maiden lady in her sixties. I did the lab work of that little hospital in those days. Patient doing beautifully. Her original percentage of sugar in twenty-four hour specimen was 8.33 per cent, the highest I have seen. I believe the world's record is about 11 per cent. Saturday's lab specimen was about 2 per cent. She was getting 40 units of insulin thrice daily—120 units a day. Sunday dinner was one meal we all made an extra effort to eat together—only an emergency could stop that; I knew of no emergency. Just as I started to pull my chair out from the dining-room table, an overwhelming compulsion came over me that I must go see that patient at once—why, I knew not. I had intended to see her when I got good and ready after dinner, but I felt I had to go then! I drove about a mile to the hospital, figuratively kicking myself all the way for being such a fool, but determined to find out what it was all about.

"I went to the room and knocked. A lady said to come in, and to my amazement, she was not my patient. I apologized and went to the hospital office where I learned that my patient had been moved to another room. I went there and knocked, received no answer, entered, and found her unconscious in insulin shock. As soon as I had given her some sugar, she came to, and then I learned her story. She was intelligent and had been told of the symptoms of approaching insulin shock—weakness, hunger, sweating, tremor, etc., and had a little bowl of sugar and a spoon on her bedside table, with instructions to take a couple of spoonfuls at once if she felt any such symptoms. When they moved her to another room, they forgot to move her sugar. Recognizing the symptoms, which with old insulin come on very fast, she looked for her sugar, couldn't find it, so got up and wandered about the room opening bureau drawers in search of it. She couldn't find any, and when she returned to bed had such severe tremors that she couldn't push the button of the call light and simply became unconscious. She had no consciousness of calling for me at the moment, even in her mind apparently, but there it is."

Yes, there it is! The lady did not remember mentally calling out for the doctor, but she may have done so. It may have been telepathy. Then again, Dr. Taylor's remarkable hunch may have been the work of one of God's busy angels. Who knows?

Peter Marshall, Chaplain of the United States Senate and pastor of the New York Avenue Presbyterian Church in Washington, once faced a grave problem. His wife, Catherine, had been very ill and faced a long convalescence. An active little son, plus a large manse to keep clean, would have taxed the strength of even a well woman. One maid after another came, stayed a short while, and then promptly succumbed to the lure of more attractive pay and more glamorous working conditions. The Marshalls wrote to orphanages and employment agencies, ran advertisements in papers, and appealed to friends, all to no avail.

In this extremity they turned to prayer. They told God that if he wanted them to keep the manse open and the family together, he could surely find them someone in that teeming city. They even set a deadline: Wednesday, September 6. If no one came by that time Mrs. Marshall would go to a rest home, the son would be placed with his grandparents, and Dr. Marshall would take a room in a hotel. Meantime, they would leave the whole matter in the hands of God and stop worrying about it.

On Friday, September 1, Alma Deane Fuller—or A. D., as she preferred to be called—joined the choir of the church. She was a reporter on one of Washington's papers and a regular attendant at Dr. Marshall's services. She had long been searching for a more intimate and complete knowledge of God, and she felt that this great Scottish preacher knew God more intimately than anyone she had ever seen. By joining the choir, she would be sure of a seat each Sunday.

Before proceeding with the rehearsal that night, the choir director felt led to tell the choir of the serious predicament existing over at the manse. Surely, he said, some one of its hundred members must know of a lady somewhere who could serve the Lord by becoming a housekeeper over there. Alma Deane felt as if he were talking directly to her. "Over and over I heard in my mind, 'A. D., why don't *you* go?' "

She did not like housework, and she knew nothing about cooking. What would her friends think if she gave up interviewing Senators and Cabinet members to become a maid? How could she live on less salary? She sat on the edge of her bed that night arguing with herself until two o'clock, but the strange compulsion would not give way.

Thus it came about that on Wednesday, the deadline, she found herself in front of the manse trying to believe it was not a dream and a bad one at that. Presently, she was sitting on the side of Mrs. Marshall's bed and saying: "Frankly, I don't even know *why* I'm here."

But God and the busy angels did! The two women talked the matter over from every angle and decided to continue to pray about it for two more weeks. During that time, A. D. discussed it with her boss. He told her she would commit professional suicide—she would, in all probability, be left far behind in the highly competitive field of journalism should she step out of it for a few months or years.

Abruptly she resigned from the paper and moved into the Marshall household as a maid. "I suddenly knew for the first time in my life," she said afterward, "what it meant to be in the right place at the right time . . . All restlessness and uncertainty left me, forever. The peace of God has never left me since that time. I know now that obedience to whatever God asks of us brings peace and a sense of rightness with the world. There is no substitute for it. That night was the beginning of a whole new life for me." *

The Marshalls were overjoyed: "We, for our part, got a more wonderful answer to our prayer than we could ever have imagined. A. D.'s four years with us were a period of

* Catherine Marshall, *A Man Called Peter* (New York: McGraw-Hill Book Co., 1951), p. 186.

spiritual adventuring and growth for Peter and me, too. He and A. D. and I became a kind of team, each of us contributing much-needed help to one another. Even A. D.'s experience on Capitol Hill was of inestimable value to Peter when he assumed the Senate chaplaincy. Links were forged between the three of us that will last through all eternity.

"Moreover, A. D. by no means committed professional suicide. In 1948, without even seeking it, she stepped into a fine position in the National Red Cross, at more than twice the salary of her old job on the Hill. That position seemed made just for her. It used every bit of experience she had ever had. Furthermore, after the interim with us, she was a lot farther up the professional ladder than she could have climbed had she spent the four years in journalism." *

At this point someone is almost sure to say that one can account for this remarkable story without any reference to influences from the world beyond. It might be said, for example, that A. D.'s deep hunger for a more intimate acquaintance with the loving presence of God was the unconscious influence that prompted her to give up her former position in order to be near Dr. Marshall. I do not subscribe to that explanation. I believe that God and his many invisible helpers in the world of spirit were at work to bring about an answer to prayer. So, let us consider another true story that seems to me to eliminate the psychological element.

It was Christmas Eve. Alexander Lake, a police reporter for the Seattle *Post Intelligencer*, sat idling at his typewriter

* *Ibid.*

in the police station press room when an overwhelming impulse sent him hurrying to Pioneer Square, three blocks down the street. He arrived just in time to knock a loaded revolver from the head of a man on the point of killing himself. The gun slithered over the grass and came to rest near a path. When the man stooped to pick it up, a well directed boot sent him sprawling.

Lake says that he glanced down the street to the illuminated hands of a big clock and idly noted that it was five minutes past seven. It crossed his mind that it was strange indeed that only five minutes earlier he had been half dozing in a warm room, and now here he was without rhyme or reason, standing over a would-be suicide with a cold drizzle dripping down his neck.

The man hid his face in his hands and sobbed out his story; of six horrible days since an officer of the law had turned the lock in his automobile-accessories store under an order of foreclosure without even letting him open the till to remove a little cash; of six days of trying to sell a gadget that nobody wanted and making exactly seventy-five cents while his wife and two children starved at home; of the tantalizing sight of the Christmas presents in the store windows that he could not buy his children while others came out of those stores laden with the things that make families happy at Christmas time.

Lake took the man to a restaurant for a bowl of soup. As they waited for the order he put in a telephone call to his office and then grabbed his hungry friend and pulled him up an alley and into a morgue garage. No time for soup now! Bill Corson, son of the coroner, was at the wheel of a car, and the three of them rolled out into the night on the way to answer a death call. Lake took two ten-dollar bills out of his wallet and shoved them into the man's pocket.

Corson drove through the mud and slush of Seattle's worst slum district to a dilapidated house filled with wailing children. All three went in. On the kitchen floor lay a large, work-worn woman. She had not been murdered. She had dropped dead at her washtub. Her Italian husband and five small children stood at the foot of the bed clutching one another. The look in the husband's eyes reflected stark tragedy. As they lifted her onto a stretcher, Jack Bryan (that is not the real name of the man who had tried to kill himself, but it will do) walked over to the sobbing father and thrust the two ten-dollar bills into his hands. Then he pleaded with Mr. Lake to take him home.

That is what they did on the way back to the morgue. Bryan jumped out and ran into his small frame cottage, followed closely by Lake. Mrs. Bryan and two little children were waiting in the kitchen. As Bryan took her in his arms and each child grabbed a leg, the wife explained: "He has been so worried and sick. Tonight when he wasn't home at seven o'clock, I knelt down and said: 'God, please take care of him and bring him home safely'—and here he is."

At that moment the tough police reporter knew why he had had an impulse to rush down to Pioneer Square at exactly seven o'clock. God had evidently wirelessed one of his guardian angels to get busy. Lake says he felt awed and humble: "Hadn't her faith in God sent me out into the dismal night to bring her husband to her?"

As the door closed behind him, he suddenly thought of the ten-dollar bills that Bryan had given to the Italian. He turned back into the house and found the father, mother, and two little children kneeling around a kitchen chair talking to God. Silently he emptied his wallet of several one-dollar bills and left them on the table. Waiting later for a cable-car, he discovered he didn't have a nickel; and so he walked back to the police station and reported to his paper, "No story"! He even kept the man's identity a secret when he wrote up the story for the *Christian Advocate* for December 20, 1951, but stated that "Jack Bryan" had made a comeback in the accessories business and was now well known up and down the entire Pacific coast.

A friend reading this chapter said: "I don't know whether I want to believe this about the busy angels; I don't want any of them watching me all the time; it would be an invasion of my privacy." I am glad she said that, because I would not want to believe that either; nor do we need to assume that they do. It seems probable that they come when sent or when some deep human need develops. After Jesus's temptation in the wilderness, we are told, "angels *came* and ministered unto him." When he was facing arrest and a mob in Gethsemane, Jesus declared that he could *ask* his Father for more than twelve legions of angels and they would be sent to protect him. Many similar instances could be cited from scripture with the same inherent implications.

One more thing. Someone is sure to ask: "If God is so good and so anxious to help mankind, why does he wait to be asked? Why doesn't he send a busy angel to help more Jack Bryans without any wives having to ask his aid?" It seems to me that such gratuitous action would destroy the beautiful intimacy of the Father-child relationship. Wise fathers do not hover protectively over their sons to shield them from all possible trouble. Sons would not grow strong and self-reliant that way. But whenever a deep and haunting *need* develops in a son's unfolding life and the son *asks* for help, the good father will go all out to help him. No one gets anything for nothing in this universe.

Jesus said: "*Ask*, and it shall be given you; *seek*, and ye shall find; *knock*, and it shall be opened unto you . . . If ye, then, being evil, know how to give good gifts unto your children, how much more shall your Father which is in heaven give good things *to them that ask him*?" (Matt. 7:7,11.)

Silent Communion for Appropriating Help from the Unseen World of Spirit

"Therefore, since we are *surrounded by so great a cloud of witnesses*, let us also lay aside every weight, and sin which clings so closely, and let us run with perseverance the race that is set before us . . ." (Hebrews 12:1, Revised Standard Version).

Think of it! I, even I, in times of great need am surrounded by invisible forces, busy angels, in the realm of spirit! It is a source of deep comfort to know that God and his helpers are never far away, but "closer than breathing and nearer than hands or feet."

CHAPTER EIGHTEEN

You Will Survive Death

It was afternoon on the first Easter day. Two men with dragging steps and sad countenances were walking along a country road from Jerusalem to the village of Emmaus. The thrilling, soul-stirring words of Jesus in the Temple earlier that same week had caught them up in a surging enthusiasm. Then had come the unbelievable news of the Nazarene's arrest, trial, and death. This was the end of their bright hopes. They were going home, sad and dejected.

As they walked they discussed the wild rumors that had been spreading over Jerusalem that very day, to the effect that Jesus was alive and had actually been seen. "But you know how credulous women are; that scarlet woman, Mary Magdalene, was the most insistent of all, for she claimed to have seen him first; but of course it couldn't be true; after all, we *saw* him die!"

So went the conversation as a stranger joined them, traveling in the same direction. He began to question them about this Nazarene and his death. His words made their hearts "burn" within them, and presently, unable longer to endure their doubt and skepticism concerning his resurrection, the stranger said: "O fools, and slow of heart to believe . . ." From that point until they reached Emmaus, the interesting stranger did the talking until about dusk they came to the village, where he was invited in to supper. "And it came to pass, as he sat at meat with them, he took bread, and blessed it, and brake, and gave to them. And their eyes were opened, and they knew him; and he vanished out of their sight." (Luke 24:25, 30–31.)

And then? Why they joined the rumor spreaders, only now they no longer called the news "rumors." They had seen and talked with Jesus! Within the hour, back over the same road to Jerusalem they flew; and burst into the upper room where the eleven disciples and some close friends were gathered and, eyes alight with joy and arms swinging like windmills, told what they had seen and heard.

Suddenly "came Jesus and stood in the midst, and saith unto them, Peace be unto you" (John 20:19). They looked at the door, locked and bolted "for fear of the Jews." It was still locked! He had come right through! Again he gave them his peace and told them to go out and tell the good news everywhere; and out they went, eleven men on the march, no longer afraid of the Jews or anybody else, to tell the most astounding story men had ever heard. Before a fortnight had passed, the radiant, living Nazarene carpenter showed himself to hundreds more until there was no longer any doubt about it—he was *alive*! On this basic fact, the infant Christian Church was founded and continues to this day!

But right here I am puzzled. The kind of thing Jesus did has been repeated in one way or another ever since. Today there are thousands of people who have been in direct or indirect contact with the world of spirit, with an innumerable company of advanced souls who have passed to the other side and remain not far removed from the world of living men: helpers and ministers of God who now and again break through the barriers of time and sense to heal and teach and to testify to the reality and closeness of the invisible world of spirit. But a single mention of these experiences brings an incredulous look and a doubtful shake of the head and most likely someone says: "Houdini didn't come back. Any good magician can fake any of those things." And if you suggest that there are counterfeit ten-dollar bills, too, but that sensible men do not on that account refuse to use good paper money, you still do not convince them of the unreasonableness of their attitude.

So, sit back, dear friends, and compose yourselves, because I propose briefly to consider some of the evidence for survival that has been manifest in recent times. Not that I advise any of you to start investigating—it is too difficult and dangerous a subject for most people to investigate on their own; but I do not think Jesus thought he was upsetting very many people when he appeared among them. It was necessary for him to establish the *fact of survival*—and so he did it!

Emanuel Swedenborg (1688–1772) was a contemporary of John Wesley. He was a great inventor, mathematician, philosopher, chemist, engineer, geologist, poet, and musician. He had made a name for himself in all of these fields when, at the age of fifty-four, his great illumination came and he experienced psychic phenomena of extraordinary character. He was in touch with numerous souls in the next world who gave him an amazing amount of detailed information about that world as well as knowledge of impending events in this world. He wrote many books that are still widely read on the subject. He had a profound influence upon such men as Tennyson, the Brownings, Ruskin, Oliver Wendell Holmes, Goethe, Coleridge, Kant, and Carlyle. On an evening late in September of 1759, he grew pale and distraught in the company of some fifteen friends in the home of William Castel as he described a great fire raging in Stockholm at that very moment three hundred miles away. He grew calm again as he finally announced, "Thank God, the fire is extinguished at the third door from my house." Two days later, letters from Stockholm confirmed every detail. Immanuel Kant was among the many who were deeply impressed after a careful investigation of all the facts.

John Wesley was deeply interested and told several friends so. In February of 1772, he received a letter from Swedenborg: "I have been informed in the world of spirits that you have a strong desire to converse with me; I shall be happy to see you if you will favor me with a visit." Wesley wrote that he would do so in about six months after his present schedule of engagements was completed. Swedenborg wrote back that the postponed meeting could not take place because he had been told he would enter the world of spirits on the twenty-ninth day of the following month; and on that day he died!

Alfred Russel Wallace (1823–1913) was the brilliant co-discoverer with Charles Darwin of the principle of evolution. When Darwin gave the world his views after a lifetime of patient and painstaking study he was greatly nonplused to have the same views expressed independently and from a far corner of the world by a man who came by them in a most novel manner. Wallace had abandoned his boyhood orthodox Christian faith at the age of fourteen and become a materialist and atheist. Then at the age of thirty-five, while he was ill with fever on the island of Ternate and temporarily unable to continue his scientific studies, there flashed upon him in a moment of brilliant insight the whole theory of evolution by natural selection as the long sought law of nature. It solved for him the problem of the origin of species and changed all his preconceived ideas. His vision included the development of life from the amoeba to man and swept on through the progress of mind, morals, and religion in the worlds of matter and of spirit. He wrote that the complete materialistic mind of his youth had changed into a spiritualistic and theistic mind with God as the Creator of all, but with a whole hierarchy of beings to help him —beings with infinite grades of power, knowledge, and wisdom. He found that "the universe requires the continuous coordinated agency of myriads of intelligences" with "man destined to a permanent progressive existence in the world of spirit." He investigated George Müller's faith orphanage, which had been supported forty-four years without any financial appeals and without the loss of a single meal. He thought the answers Müller received to prayer did not come from a solitary God sitting at a cosmic telephone exchange but rather resulted from the cooperation of spiritual beings in a vast unseen kingdom of God. His influence grew to such proportions that he was finally buried in Westminster Abbey.

In 1942, after carefully investigating the facts in the life story of Edgar Cayce of Virginia Beach, Virginia, Thomas Sugrue published them in *There Is a River.* This is a remarkable book. Cayce, who died in 1945, was a simple, honest, uneducated, devout Christian. When he was about twenty-one years of age, he learned that he had rare psychic gifts. If he himself or some friend were suffering from any ailment, he could go to sleep with this problem on his mind. Presently he would start talking, or rather, some personality in the world of spirit would talk through him, diagnosing the disease and prescribing for it. The phraseology was always that of a well trained physician, although Cayce himself knew absolutely nothing about medicine. By this means he healed his wife of an advanced case of tuberculosis, and his son of threatened blindness.

My friend Sherwood Eddy, author of the challenging and valuable book *You Will Survive After Death* was just beginning a ten-year study of psychic phenomena, and the testimony of five doctors convinced him he should investigate the work of Edgar Cayce. He went to Virginia Beach in May of 1938 and stayed for some time. Again and again, as he watched, this strange man engaged in a period of earnest prayer before falling into a self-induced sleep or trance. Mrs. Cayce and a secretary always sat by to take down his readings. Eddy listened to detailed diagnoses and elaborate technical prescriptions from a simple man who, in his waking state, knew absolutely nothing about medicine. In forty years, Cayce had given readings in more than fifteen thousand cases, some of them present, others at a great distance. Dr. Eddy wrote to many of the physicians who had come to Mr. Cayce for help. Their answers showed that Cayce's advice had resulted in more cures than could be expected from the foremost experts in various fields of medicine. David Khan of New York City, wrote to Dr. Eddy that he had seen or known of three thousand readings by Edgar Cayce over a period of twenty-five years and the results were good in all of them.

This man never charged a nickel for any of his work, and so he was always poor. He told Dr. Eddy that early in his career he had foolishly consented to use his power to foretell the results of some horse races in Cincinnati for a man. The first day the man won $50. The next day he made $1,800 in five races, then $15,000 and finally $200,000. This easy money went to the man's head, and he started drinking and living riotously and ended in an insane asylum. Cayce never again allowed his gift to be used selfishly.

While I was preparing to write this chapter, my old friend Howard Thurman of the Church of All Peoples in San Francisco came to stay a night. He said that he had been devoting an hour a week for two years to teaching a badly crippled woman about God. She was paralyzed from the waist down as a result of an accident. She told Dr. Thurman that she had gone to Edgar Cayce for a reading; he told her then that her accident had caused a small bone to lodge precariously across certain nerves near her spine, and he advised an operation. Two specialists took X-rays and stated the picture showed no such bone position. Both men, in succession, refused even an exploratory operation. She went to a third surgeon, and he agreed to try. Imagine his surprise to find the exact condition that Cayce had described!

Although space is not available here to review further the remarkable material in Sherwood Eddy's book, *You Will Survive After Death*, I heartily commend it to all. He was in Iowa City before it was published, and I talked with him at length about his ten years of study that preceded publication. It is the sanest and best balanced book of its kind that I have ever read. Through close friends who have unusual psychic gifts he had talked at length with all seven members of his family who were in the next world; and the information he received was highly evidential and convincing. Nevertheless, he did not advise the average interested layman to dabble or experiment in this field. On the other hand he believed that we can all safely inform ourselves on the results of such experimentation and thereby obtain an unshakable faith in the glorious fact of a future life. That was undoubtedly Jesus's purpose in his many post-resurrection appearances.

River of Years gives us a glimpse of the late beloved Dr. Joseph Fort Newton's deep interest in psychic phenomena.

He was acquainted with Pearl Curran, the wholesome and delightful person through whom the remarkable words of Patience Worth were given to the world. Patience Worth was a soul in the kingdom of spirit who used Mrs. Curran as an amanuensis to give the world poetry and stories of rarest beauty which Dr. Newton avers would have been utterly impossible for Mrs. Curran to produce by herself: "Dr. Prince, research officer of the Boston Society for Psychic Research, studied the case for months, comparing the poetry of Patience Worth with that of Tennyson, Arnold and Wordsworth, not to her disadvantage."

He continues: "One of the stories was a full length life of Jesus, telling how a Greek slave girl gave birth to a child on the night on which Jesus was born—only her child was the incarnation of Hate, as Jesus was of Love; hence the title, 'A Sorry Tale.' The two lives ran parallel; their paths crossed—and the child of the slave girl was the unrepentant thief who died on one of the three crosses outside the city gate. Such was the literary device; the version of the Sermon on the Mount in the story was a thing of unearthly beauty—I read it with a bowed mind." He concludes: "My friend, Mrs. Curran, was as much astonished as anyone else at the stories and poems she produced." *

In closing, let me confess that while I have no psychic gifts I have been tremendously impressed by the mountain of evidence that I have come across through years of wide reading in favor of the reality of an unseen world. The

* Joseph Fort Newton, *River of Years: An Autobiography* (Philadelphia: J. B. Lippincott Co., 1946), p. 183.

writer of Hebrews graphically recounts the exploits of innumerable men of faith who have lived heroically and passed on to their eternal reward. "Therefore, let us too, with such a crowd of witnesses about us, throw off every impediment and the entanglement of sin and run with determination the race for which we are entered" (Hebrews 12:1, Goodspeed translation).

We are indeed surrounded by a cloud of witnesses. In the bleak wastes of the Antarctic, Captain Robert Scott is writing with frozen fingers. After incredible hardships and heartbreak, all his companions save one are gone—and that one sits silent upon the snow. It is the end, and Scott knows it. Is he overcome with resentment and fear at that cold, lonely and dreadful moment? Let him answer: "As we sit here in this barren waste, we think of home and our loved ones. We are very lonely in these last hours. Yet, *we are cheered*, for it seems there are three of us here, not just two. It is Jesus, and his presence comforts us. All along he seems to have journeyed with us. He faced death alone and unafraid. *So do we.* God bless our dear friends." Four years later, a rescue party found the body of Captain Scott—and under his head his own quiet testimony of the presence of one of the cloud of witnesses.

Silent Communion for Facing the Great Divide

"Let not your heart be troubled: ye believe in God, believe also in me. In my Father's house are many mansions

. . . I go to prepare a place for you . . . that where I am, there ye may be also." (John 14:1–3.)

This I believe with all my heart and I am not afraid of life's greatest and most thrilling adventure.

CHAPTER NINETEEN

Conscience and Crucifixion

"And sitting down they watched him there" (Matt. 27:36). Such is the brief, graphic, searing description of the action of the soldiers who had just nailed Jesus to his cross. After all, they were tired. It had been a long, hot walk from Pilate's palace out to Golgotha. They had done their duty as they saw it. Their consciences were clear. Now they would rest a bit before returning to the city. Strange man, that, taking his own death so quietly and praying for the very men who hung him there: why not watch him die!

Near by were high churchmen, members of the Jewish Sanhedrin who had demanded his death. They were telling themselves that their consciences were clear, too. After all, this Jesus had openly flouted their religious customs and beliefs; he had violated the Sabbath day; he had eaten with publicans and sinners without washing his hands; he had encouraged immorality by forgiving the harlot Mary Magdalene, when Moses had specified that such should be stoned; he had been false to hopes of Jewish nationalism by preaching against bloody revolution—even had gone so far as to preach love for one's enemies when the Mosaic law proclaimed an eye for an eye and a tooth for a tooth. Thus, he was no believer in the Bible. No! This man was destroying the old landmarks and changing everything; it was a matter of conscience to put him to death!

What crimes have been committed through the centuries for conscience' sake! In Moses' day, a Hebrew could sell his own daughter into slavery with no feeling of guilt—it was the law (Exodus 21:7); one who hit or cursed his father or mother could be put to death (Exodus 21:15, 17); he might sell spoiled meat to foreigners but not to Hebrews (Deut. 14:21). Precise laws made these things common custom which the people believed to be *right.*

What is conscience? "Conscience," says *Webster's New International Dictionary*, is the "sense or consciousness of the moral goodness or blameworthiness of one's own conduct, intentions, or character, together with a feeling of obligation to do or be that which is recognized as good." It is that innate sense of oughtness to follow the right course of conduct when we understand what that course should be. Violation of this inborn sense of oughtness brings feelings of guilt which may be serious even to the extent of mental derangement.

Note this fact well, however: we are born with a conscience, but we are not born with a knowledge of what is right and wrong. The average conscience is made up of family opinions, neighborhood prejudices, and the current superstitions and biases of the people with whom we live and work. David Seabury puts it thus: "We know that when we become enmeshed in an environment and have taken on its thought patterns, it is difficult for us to open our minds to attitudes in wide contrast with those to which we have become habituated. This rigidity is caused by what are technically known as coenotropes; that is, centers of prejudice and ideas toward life on which the mind has become set, to which it attributes special values and toward which it turns as inevitably as steel is drawn to a magnet." Then he gives us this punch line: "The delusion that one's conscience, as the word is commonly understood, will reveal what is right and what is wrong is a coenotrope to which deranged minds will hold and for which they will fight as fiercely as for their very egos." *

This fact holds true in the field of religion. When a child is emotionally conditioned to a fear-based religion, it is very difficult for the light of reason to change him. I personally struggled for many years with religious coenotropes. I was brought up in a fundamentalist environment and inherited certain beliefs about the Bible, salvation, the Virgin Birth, heaven, hell, the Trinity, and related dogma. In Boston University School of Theology, I was led into honest study and inquiry that threw a flood of new light on these dogmas. I came to see that a lot of man-made theological mumbo-jumbo had been superimposed upon the simple, nontheological, radiant Christ through the centuries: viewpoints

* David Seabury, *How Jesus Heals Our Minds Today* (Boston: Little, Brown & Co., 1940), pp. 182–183.

that I came to feel did violence to what Jesus himself thought and taught. Slowly my whole theological outlook changed; it was like sweating blood to rid myself of my coenotropes.

I finally wrote a book about it all, *Something to Stand On*, which is now in its eighth printing; and the wide reader audience has brought a flood of mail to my desk. Almost all the letters express gratitude, but a few are from people determined that all the arguments in the world from now until Doomsday shall not change their preconceived ideas in the slightest degree. To them the new light that I tried to throw on the Bible and on the teachings of Jesus is all wrong and I myself am a fearful heretic.

Comes then this question: if we are not born with a knowledge of right and wrong, if the conscience is no true guide in the matter, if well intentioned people are often to be found persecuting others whom the test of time and true scholarship prove to be right, how can we ever be sure of what is right and wrong?

Here is the answer as I see it: Jesus taught that the most precious value in the universe is the human soul. Man, made in the image of God, is of eternal worth. Any viewpoint or any act that tends to destroy spiritual capacity is wrong; any viewpoint or act that tends to integrate, ennoble, and build up spiritual capacity is right. It is, to me, as simple as that.

At the age of twelve I heard a preacher say from his pulpit that it was a mark of sinful pride to wear a necktie. He himself wore a celluloid collar which he cleaned occasionally with the swish of a damp rag—but he wore no tie. I thought he looked terrible. Still, he was an authority on hell and how hot the place could be if you died having pride in your heart. He should know, being a preacher.

One night I had a toothache and lay staring into the darkness. Suddenly a bright idea came to me. I had no hope that that tooth would stop aching of itself. So I prayed: "O God, if you will stop my tooth from aching right now, I'll take it as a sign from you that it is your will that I shouldn't wear a tie ever again." The old tooth kept right on aching as I knew and hoped it would, and the next morning I put on the reddest tie I had. Red has been my favorite color ever since! I know now that wearing a tie is right and is not a sign of sin at all. Reasonable pride in one's appearance is a good thing. It satisfies one's esthetic sense. Omission of a necktie would have caused me to suffer for being freakish in appearance. I probably would have developed an inferiority complex and thus decreased spiritual capacity and wholeness.

It was not long afterwards that I had another severe bout with conscience. I had been at Sunday school and church one fine spring morning. That afternoon a neighbor lad put up his croquet set and invited me to a game. We were enjoying ourselves immensely when my mother called me home. She said it was wicked to play on Sunday, and reminded me of a sermon I had recently heard on that very theme. I got out the big family Bible and looked at vivid pictures of people plunging into the flames of hell directly from the hands of an angry God; and I prayed to be forgiven. My conscience really hurt!

Today I could play a game of croquet on a Sunday afternoon and enjoy it with no pangs of remorse. The fresh air and the stimulating competition would benefit me physically and spiritually. This new viewpoint stems directly from a careful and open-minded study of the teaching of Jesus. He was accused by the churchmen of his day of breaking the law when he healed a man on the Sabbath. He applied the rule we stated a moment ago and said it was lawful to do good on the Sabbath, rule or no rule. His disciples picked wheat and ate it on the Sabbath. He said they were not to be condemned. After all, they were hungry even on the Sabbath. With one sentence he cut through the shallow coenotrope surrounding Sabbath observance: "The sabbath was made for men, and not man for the sabbath."

Jesus was a pattern breaker and a fighter of outworn convention; he repudiated stereotyped sanctions because he believed we must choose between two diametrically opposed attitudes of life: externalism and internalism. In determining the difference between right and wrong, we must shape conduct on an understanding of the eternal verities, on what tends to destroy personality values and what tends to enhance and integrate them.

Says David Seabury: "No man is good in the true sense whose face is not joyous, whose eyes are not merry, whose laugh is not full, whose glance is not direct, whose ways are not spontaneous. The thinner his lips, the narrower his nature. A yellow skin and a bilious heart are as one. And as for those who move about in austere seriousness, we know that many of them are hypocrites." *

Our Pilgrim forebears never celebrated Christmas. They thought this holiday was unscriptural if not downright pagan, and so they worked all day. But in 1621 some new arrivals said it "wente against their consciences" to work on Christmas. Governor Bradford "tould them that if they made it a mater of conscience, he would spare them till they were better informed. So he led-away ye rest and left them; but when they came home at noone from their worke, he found them in ye streete at play, openly; some pitching ye barr, and some at stoole-ball, and such like sports. So he went to them, and tooke away their implements, and tould them that was against his conscience, that they should play & others worke. If they made ye keeping of it mater of devotion, let them kepe their houses, but ther should be no gameing or revelling in ye streets."

These Pilgrim Fathers were a grim lot. They revolted against any display of joy as something akin to the foul court life of England's dissolute kings. In childhood they were emotionally conditioned to the point of view that celebrations and joy on Christmas were wrong. And if they *thought* they were wrong, they were wrong for them, until such time as they could be induced to accept new light.

When Philip II of Spain lay dying he was troubled in conscience lest the heavenly Power should censure him because he had not killed enough heretics! He had ordered

* *Ibid.*, p. 180.

many a good man done to death with the unspeakable engines of torture used in the Inquisition. Was Philip right to be so troubled?

Manifestly not. He lived in a credulous age in which the Roman Catholic Church taught that a man was saved or lost according as he believed exactly what the church taught. Philip thought that a "heretic" tortured into accepting the church's viewpoint could be saved.

Not long before, Martin Luther had become convinced that men are "justified by faith" in God, and that no church or priest holds the keys of the kingdom of heaven. The New Testament does not teach that we are saved through a system of beliefs, though what one believes is surely of great importance. Loving God and one's neighbor, as Jesus clearly portrayed, is the key to salvation. Philip was an ignorant, superstitious monarch in sad need of enlightenment. His conscience needed training.

Edward J. Flynn, long-time political boss of New York City, defends boss rule in his book *You're the Boss.* He says that many years ago a committee came to him from upstate New York with the information that the Republicans were buying votes for $1.50 apiece. If he would up the ante to $1.75 he could have those votes for *his* candidate. He gave them the money, but his candidate was defeated anyway by a large margin. Then, he says, that same candidate "blossomed out in a new Buick automobile!"

Clearly Flynn regards the man as immoral: instead of using Flynn's money to buy votes, he kept it and bought himself a car! Flynn does not question the rightness or wrongness of buying votes nor the effect of such action upon the characters of men. He is not concerned about what happens to democracy when such practices are widespread. No, he lost through a double cross, and that proves that the *other* fellow was immoral! Flynn has no personality yardstick for determining right and wrong. He, therefore, has no basis for a trained conscience.

In his fascinating book, *The Life and Times of Rembrandt*, Hendrik van Loon gives us another interesting illustration. Van Loon's great-great-grandfather was the friend and physician of Rembrandt. When Hendrickje, Rembrandt's common-law wife, was admitted to Dr van Loon's hospital to bear Rembrandt a son, she was in such pain that she begged the doctor to poison her and end it all. Anesthetics were unknown in the middle of the seventeenth century, but this daring physician was secretly experimenting with a hemp derivative which put people to sleep during an operation without any serious after effects.

One dose of the drug and Hendrickje mercifully forgot her pain. The child was born, the mother was soon home again, and all was well. Or perhaps we should say that all would have been well had the nurse not started telling the pious, God-fearing church people of Amsterdam about the drug that killed pain. A week later, the Reverand Zebediah preached his famous sermon on "Childbearing Without God's Curse." He shouted that this doctor was overturning the plan of God by taking away the pain God had intended. Soon the whole town was denouncing "this libertine and Arminian who pretended to be wiser than God."

Then one night, an orderly mob of several hundred men and women gathered at the hospital in the middle of the night, carried the eighteen patients into the street, and burned the place to the ground. As they went home and to bed, each one no doubt felt he had satisfied the demands of conscience. They had preserved the plan of God for the savage inroads of pain at childbirth!

Reminds me of the mistress of one of the great mansions in England, who, determined to demonstrate the mellowing influence of the "true" Christmas spirit, stopped reading the story of the Nativity in the Gospel of Luke long enough to say to one of the servants: "Wilson, this is Christmas Eve. See that none but our *best* cheese is put into the mouse traps tonight."

The burning of Dr. van Loon's hospital demonstrates how easily the opinions of the crowd color our thinking. Especially so, when the clergy, in their pious ignorance, preach sermons about something from "the Word of God." The literal interpretation of the Bible has often stopped the clock of progress for long periods of time. The clergy threatened Galileo with torture unless he would retract his statement that the world was round. Did not the Bible say it was flat? And even to this day, many conscientious clergymen stoutly maintain that the earth was made in six literal days. Does not the Bible say so? Many young people in universities go through a terrific struggle with their consciences for this very reason. Confronted with courses of study that teach the evolutionary hypothesis, they feel that they may be doubting God if they accept it.

What we need above everything else in the world is the *open, honest, questing mind*; the mind with its critical faculties alive and working; the mind that keeps its yardstick of personality values handy at all times; the mind that is unafraid of new truths, unconcerned over the effect of new wine in old bottles! An intelligent, educated conscience is the growing edge of any dynamic life: a growing edge that easily becomes blunted when fear of public opinion is allowed to rob us of our soul's integrity.

An intelligent, trained conscience can get us into plenty of trouble, but that is the high price of progress. Jesus defied the whole false system of externalism in religion in favor of internalism. *It cost him his life.* Sir Thomas More, friend of Henry VIII, used his personality yardstick in the fierce debate about the rightness or wrongness of Henry's desire to marry Anne Boleyn and decided it was wrong. Even the threat of death in the Tower of London was powerless to make him approve the sensual monarch's wishes. On the way to the block, he expressed pity for the jeering mob whose consciences had already ceased to exist.

As they impaled his head upon a pole on London Bridge, the silent lips could truthfully have said: "This is infinitely preferable to the dulling of the keen cutting edge of my conscience. I enter the realm of the blessed with my personality intact and all the real values of existence conserved." With Paul, he could joyfully have shouted: "I have fought a good fight, I have finished my course, I have kept the faith: Henceforth there is laid up for me a crown of righteousness, which the Lord, the righteous judge, shall give me at that day."

Silent Communion for Keeping a Growing Edge in Life

"Ye shall know the truth, and the truth will make you free" (John 8:32).

"For the law was given by Moses, but grace [graciousness] and truth came by Jesus Christ" (John 1:17).

Because all truth is God's truth, I am unafraid of where it may lead me. My critical faculties are wide open to an honest examination of all sides of every question, including those in the field of religion. There is a keen, growing edge to my life.

CHAPTER TWENTY

The Measure of a Man

There are many jokes about men who die and go to heaven only to be stopped at the pearly gates for some pointed questioning from St. Peter. I do not hold a theology that admits of any literal interpretation of Matthew 16:19 where Peter is given the keys of the kingdom of heaven. But I have often speculated about what I would do if Peter actually had those keys and he should ask me (don't worry —there isn't a chance!) to assist him in working out a set of questions that should be put to all comers.

There are some things I would not bother about: things like a man's ancestry, college degrees, bank account, size of his home, the kind of car he drove, what he was president of, or even his theology. These may be important, but I would skip them all. I should want the answers to just four questions, and I would stake my final judgment of the man on the revelations thereby uncovered. I am assuming that everything a man does or says or thinks in life leaves an indelible impression upon the supersensitive photographic plate of the universe, and that I should automatically have access to this minute record.

First: How fearless was he in the face of manifest duty? At regular intervals we suffer from a plethora of moral boondoggling in high places. It is probably true that the great majority of our public servants are men of integrity. But it is also true that there are always men on the national and local levels who are utterly faithless to their public trusts. No government and no business can be any stronger than the characters of the men in places of power. Sometimes the tide of wrongdoing runs so strong that it takes a rare fearlessness to stand foursquare against it.

One day in the Illinois state legislature a member gave a stirring address on the subject, "Put Down Lincoln." When he had finished, Lincoln arose and said: "I would rather die than change my views and by that change obtain office." On another occasion when he was being urged to forget his convictions in a political deal, he cried: "You may burn my body and scatter the ashes to the four winds of heaven; you may drag my soul down into the pit; but you will never get me to support what I believe to be wrong." No wonder he lost so many political battles; but what a deep impression he was making on the eternal and cosmic photographic plate of the universe!

Forever invigorating and refreshing is the story of the fearless Queen Esther. You will recall that the scheming and wicked Haman had risen to such favor with King Ahasuerus that all the Jews scattered throughout the kingdom were forced to do obeisance before him; all, that is, except proud old Mordecai. So Haman trumped up some false charges against the Jews and obtained the king's permission to hang them all. The beautiful Queen Esther, herself a Jew, undertook irrevocably to save her people by telling the king of the plot.

But how to gain an interview without being invited? It was the law that if anyone, even the queen, approached the royal presence without an invitation, he should be put to death, and Esther's friends warned her of this. Her answer has rung down the intervening centuries: "I go in unto the king . . . and if I perish, I perish." Fearlessness in the face of manifest duty! And, of course, she won, and Haman was hanged on the very gallows he had prepared for Mordecai!

Second: What kind of steward of time, talent, and substance was he? Let's see his check stubs for the last twenty years of his life, when he was old enough to know what money was for. Now let's have the exact percentages of what he gave away, and what he kept for himself. At this point it is probable that even St. Peter will occasionally look startled at the number of "good" people who keep 99 per cent for themselves and give away the rest.

President Virgil Hancher of the University of Iowa told one day of a conversation he had with a certain woman. "I go to church only two or three times a year," she said. "I don't get anything out of it." He asked her if she played golf. When she replied in the affirmative he asked how often she played. "Oh, about three times a week," she said. "It's a lot of fun." "But don't you think you'd get more out of church if you went oftener and put more into it?" asked Dr. Hancher.

More than half of Jesus's parables dealt with material prosperity. "Fools" was the harsh word he used to characterize the men who filled their barns to overflowing in order to "eat, drink and be merry," the while their souls perished for lack of spiritual food. So, let's have a look at the check stubs.

One New Year's Day a well known man sat at his library desk with a pen in his hand and a smile upon his face. He wrote checks that totaled $645,000 to a lot of people to whom he owed not a thin dime—legally. But Reuben H. Donnelley had had a remarkable childhood training by a mother whose integrity and sense of stewardship were rare indeed.

One story told to the sensitive lad by his mother at bedtime after he had said his prayers made an indelible impression on him. It was the tale of the little ermine. Its fur, she told him, is brown in summer but snow-white in winter. This is the beautiful white fur used on the robes of royalty as a symbol of honor, of nobleness of mind, an allegiance to all that is just and right.

And she vividly portrayed the wonderful character of the ermine; its pride in the spotless purity of its white coat—so great that hunters would try to drive the little animal toward the mud, knowing that it would stop and suffer itself to be captured rather than soil its garment. Then, this wise mother told Reuben of the great dreams she had about his future; of her prayer that in the business world he might be a man of justice and honor and truth, willing to suffer financial loss rather than do an unprincipled thing.

Well, Reuben grew to manhood and went into business.

He became a stockbroker in Wall Street. He made a lot of money honestly and then, as often happens, he went broke. He was forced into bankruptcy and finally paid off hundreds of his investors at 27 cents on the dollar. This hurt Reuben worse than it did the investors. They had lost good money through his questionable judgment, and some of them were poor people.

Then, Reuben H. Donnelley invented the classified telephone directory, where one can find a man by his business or profession. It made him a fortune in a very few years. That is how he came to write all those checks one New Year's Day. He remembered the ermine story and his mother's dream for him. Legally, he was not responsible. Morally, he felt obligated to pay both principal and interest of every dollar anyone had lost with him. His first check was to a scrubwoman in Chicago—a check for $10,000. Reuben Donnelley was giving a magnificent account of his stewardship.

Third question: How much did he really *love* even "the least of these my little ones"? In giving the Great Commandment, after first telling men to love God, Jesus declared the second half was like the first: *Love your neighbor* as you love yourself. As John said: "Love is of God, and he who loves is born of God and knows God. He who does not love does not know God; for God is love." Let's not bother with the man's testimony in prayer meeting; let's have the *record*! Mussolini was at least honest in his barbarity. He used to say, "We wish to hear no more about brotherhood," and he met the fate that absence of brotherhood aways brings.

Dr. Richard Salter Storrs of the Church of the Pilgrims in Brooklyn was asked by a small boy to come and see his sister who was gravely ill. Entering a wretched one-room tenement in the slums, he found a sad situation indeed. The mother had died; the worthless father had disappeared; and a frail fifteen-year-old sister had taken over the task of breadwinner and mother. She had worked her fingers to the bone and now lay dying of tuberculosis induced by malnutrition and overfatigue.

As Dr. Storrs attempted to comfort her, she kept asking: "How will God know that I belong to him when I come?" She was worried about her ignorance of theological matters; she had been so busy loving and serving her poor little brood that she had not gone to church often. Dr. Storrs looked down at the little crucified creature, saw on the ragged blanket the shriveled and work-worn fingers that had kept the dishes washed and the meager meals cooked, and he said: "Show him your hands. He'll know then you belong to him." Yes, let's have the plain, unvarnished record of the brother's loving *deeds*.

From the Act of Horodlo (A.D. 1413) and inspired by Queen Jadwiga of Poland comes this penetrating insight:

Nor can that endure which has not its foundations upon love.
For love alone diminishes not, but shines with its own light;
Makes an end of discord, softens the fires of hate,
Restores peace in the world, brings together the sundered,

Redresses wrong, aids all and injures none;
And who so invokes its aid will find peace and safety,
And have no fear of future ill.

Finally, let us ask: How did he take heartbreak and suffering? Did it *break* him? or *make* him? Because, if he whined and whimpered when the blows came, without faith in God or man or in himself, he became a dead weight in the water of life, dragging himself and others down into the depths. But if he kept his faith, if he believed that all things work together for good *to them that love God*, if he accepted trouble as a challenge, if as someone has said he took the lemons that life threw at him and started a lemonade stand, he floated serenely over the roughest shoals and came at last to his desired haven.

It has been eleven years since the comedian Joe E. Brown lost his son, Captain Don Brown. As far as Joe was concerned, the sun rose and set in that fine lad. He was handsome, blond, healthy, and strong, with a quick mind and a flair for leadership. At U.C.L.A. he had been president of the student body and student colonel of the R.O.T.C. force of 3,000 boys. He was a competent and careful pilot of his plane, but he had no way of knowing that some enemy of his country had sabotaged the engine in such a way as to cause the propellers to stop over dangerous country. But they did stop, and Don was killed.

I can think of no more tragic and arduous assignment than for a professional funny man suddenly to be confronted with the loss of such a son. How could he ever laugh and make others feel happy and carefree when his own heart was broken? At the moment, Joe was in Detroit playing in "The Show-Off." For twenty hours he was in violent rebellion. "There is no God," he told himself. "If there were one, he couldn't have let this happen. He couldn't!"

Then a strange thing happened. He wandered out to the airport and saw ten boys in uniform with shoulder patches that indicated they belonged to Don's outfit. Joe Brown began to talk with them and suddenly felt that they too were his boys. "When you have lost your own son," he says, "all other lads become your sons." That thought was finally to carry him into every theater of World War II. Don was gone, but here were all these other boys fighting the battle for a free world: boys whose parents loved them as much as Joe had loved Don; boys who were thousands of miles away from home, often lonely and ill; boys many of whom would die as Don had died. As his great heart went out to them, he felt that they should have all the laughs that he, Joe E. Brown, could possibly pack into an hour's entertainment.

Then Joe developed a severe case of sciatica, brought on by long trips, irregular hours, loss of sleep, and extremes of heat and cold. He insisted on keeping his schedule just the same even when he had to be carried from place to place in an ambulance. The boys were not to know: they had troubles of their own. So Joe made his driver dump him out a couple of miles from each camp. Summoning all the grit he could muster, he would come clowning into camp just as though he enjoyed every blessed moment of it.

One day Joe walked into a hospital ward where a boy lay dying—so they said. But when Joe put on his famous grin the boy was overjoyed. "You came to see me. That shows there's somebody looking after me, so now I'm going to get well." Something happened to Joe also when that brave and confident testimony was given, and he suddenly felt that he too was going to get well; but he did not know how remarkable his experience was going to be.

One night on Christmas Island, as he gazed out over a sea of faces, he "was just busting to give those kids more fun than any one man could possibly give them." He had not danced for months: he could not. But at that moment he remembered a crazy old dance he used to do in vaudeville—several dances rolled into one that carried him all over the stage like a whirling dervish—and before he knew it, he had plunged into that dance! The boys howled with glee, and when it was over and Joe stood mopping his brow he suddenly realized that his sciatica and his pain were gone—gone for good. "I don't know what faith is or how you get it," says Joe, "but one thing I am sure of: *I trust God with my whole life.*" Well, Joe, my friend, *that is faith*, and it is the genuine article, too.

Joe Brown lost a wonderful son. That is sorrow and trouble spelled in capital letters, but it is also heartache such as millions of others have faced. The difference between Joe and many of these millions is the difference that automatically takes a man's measure. Instead of letting his sorrow swamp him, instead of allowing his mind to focus so intently on his loss that it ruined his life, Joe Brown went over onto the positive side of his trouble and made it serve the many thousands of homesick boys all over the world. As he moved through one tragic hospital ward after another, flashing his infectious grin, he often felt that Don was by his side. He kept going so that Don would be proud of him. And in the process, through the blessed operation of this faith-hope-love-work technique, he himself was healed in both his soul and his pain-racked body.

Could God have prevented the death of Captain Don Brown? The answer is No, not without changing the whole scheme of the universe and thus depriving us of our precious freedom of choice. Don's plane had been sabotaged by some enemy of our country. The man who did it was exercising his freedom of choice to do an evil thing. All of us, made in the image of God, are free to choose either evil or good. Take away that choice and we should become automatons with no means of growing strong, sturdy souls. We become morally a little weaker every time we make an evil choice, and a little stronger when we choose the good.

But God can use what he does not choose! It was not his will that Don should be killed. When it happened, however, a loving ever-present Spirit was ready to fill and use a grief-stricken father to benefit thousands of other boys and, in the process, to deepen, broaden, and ennoble the personality of Joe E. Brown. His inner splendor was released to bless and heal countless numbers of the sons of men.

There we have the four questions I would put to all men were St. Peter to ask me to help him determine the status of those who come knocking at the pearly gates:

1. How fearless were you, brother, in the face of manifest duty? 2. What kind of steward were you of time, talent, and earthly goods? 3. How much did you really *love* men as evidenced by the record? 4. How did you handle heartbreak and suffering?

Please note that in every single question lies the implication of freedom of choice. Our destinies are in our own frail hands. But "behind the dim unknown standeth God within the shadow, keeping watch above His own." There will be times of testing when the skies of the soul are like lead and God seems very far away and uncaring; days when we seem to be walking through the valley of the shadow of death, alone and unsupported. Then, we shall do well to remember the lonely cry of Jesus as he hung dying on the cross: "My God, my God, why hast thou forsaken me?" God's answer came to Jesus and to the whole world as quietly and as brilliantly as the rising of the sun on Easter morning. This experience high-lights the glory of man's greatest freedom: the freedom to *choose* to trust a loving God in the face of life's greatest sorrows, to prove that "all things work together for good to those who love God."

Silent Communion for Measuring My Potential Strength

I am resolved, by the strength of the God-Power within, to be fearless at all times; to be a generous steward of time, talent, and substance; truly to love all men by demonstrating unbreakable good will; to face heartbreak and suffering as Christ did in the confidence that, quietly borne, it will add to the final beauty and harmony of life's pattern.

CHAPTER TWENTY-ONE

Faith, Love, Zest, and Grandma Reynolds

There are fifteen million people in America today who are over sixty-five years of age. Millions of them are getting old largely because they *think* they are through with life. Sixty-five is the generally accepted age of retirement, and so many of these dear people spend the last decade of active life preparing to step into the role of an old person. Other millions are old at thirty and forty and fifty.

So, come along with me for a two-day visit in Hollywood with Grandma Reynolds the very week she reaches ninety. Catch the contagion of her youthful, love-inspired, faith-motivated life, and I'll wager you'll go away with a zest for living that will surprise your friends as well as yourself. You'll never be the same again!

When I walked up to the plain little cottage that is her home, there was a sign on the door: "Yes, I'm home! Ring hard and keep on ringing and I'll soon be here. I thank you. Grandma Reynolds." I rang, and she came to greet me with both hands outstretched and a "God bless you" on her lips. Her face is deeply lined with the scars of battle, but the radiant faith that has been hers for nearly a century has tilted all those lines upward until she seems to be always smiling even when she is in complete repose.

She is the most self-forgetful and outgoing personality I have ever seen. For two days we traveled all over Hollywood and Los Angeles meeting friends who have known her through the years. How they love her! Taking my arm, she stepped off with me at a brisk pace, uphill and down, on a long walk to the bus. People on the bus or car were always recognizing this lively old grandmother of the films. She greeted each one like an old friend with that contagious smile and, like as not, ended up by giving an autographed copy of the latest story of her accomplishments. She always seemed to have one more of these tucked away in her handbag. She said, "God bless you," every time she parted from these new friends, nor was it ever hackneyed or commonplace. She meant it from the bottom of her stout heart.

After ten hours of steady going, I suggested that we go and see her latest film, *Lydia Bailey*, if she wasn't too tired. "Fiddlesticks, this has been an easy day," she said. "Let's go. What are we waiting for?" In the theater a twelve-year-old boy in front of us turned around, peered at her, and said, "Aren't you Grandma Reynolds? Aren't you the grandma in this picture?" When she admitted her identity, he leaned way back for a good look, and said, "Gee, you're the first movie star I've ever seen in real life! Gee!" She leaned forward for a chat and asked him several questions and then told me to put down his name and address. The next morning she wrote him a note in a firm clear script and sent him an autographed magazine article full of pictures. "You never can tell how much a little thing like this will help," she said.

Adeline de Walt was born in 1862 on a farm near Vinton, Iowa. One of a large family, she pitched hay, milked cows, drove a team, and in general did a man's work. She was born with a deep love of dramatics in her very bones, and as a little girl she dreamed of some day becoming a great actress. For one reason and another it was necessary to postpone her plans for seventy years; but she never gave them up. At eighty she was finally ready, and in the last ten years she has played an amazing variety of grandmother roles in over thirty films, including *Shadow of the Thin Man* with William Powell and Myrna Loy, *Tuttles of Tahiti* with Charles Laughton, *Street of Chance* with Burgess Meredith, *Happy Land* with Don Ameche, *Pony Soldier* with Tyrone Power, *Going My Way*, *A Tree Grows in Brooklyn*, *The Corn Is Green*, *Lydia Bailey*, *Here Comes the Groom*, and *Kim.*

On the Vinton farm, her understanding mother was as tender and considerate as her father was harsh. Recognizing the worth of Adeline's dreams, the mother gave her a penny a dozen for all the stray eggs she found outside the henhouse. So, with the savings from 6,000 eggs, she promptly bought a good dictionary, and the works of Shakespeare in one volume. She memorized many of the words in her dictionary and, standing on a knoll in the cornfield, repeated them in such a dramatic manner that she imagined the corn stalks waved majestically in dignified assent.

From that day she fed her hungry soul on the noblest thoughts of the ages as she plowed through volume after volume, running the wisdom of the seers through her own mind until it left its stamp upon her personality.

That volume of Shakespeare paid off, too. At the age of sixty-four, when most people think they are about through, she was ready to start working her way through college. Her children, for whom she had postponed her own dreams, were educated and out on their own. So, she enrolled in the University of California and put herself through by tutoring students in French, keeping one lesson ahead of those she coached.

The drama professor took a very dim view of an "old woman" enrolling in his classes. He coldly told her that she would have to pass a public audition and compete with eighteen-year-olds who had fire and imagination. So, she went back to her beloved Shakespeare and chose a scene from *Antony and Cleopatra.* I can hear her emotionally charged voice now as, facing the professor and his inexperienced eighteen-year-olds, she cried: "Age cannot wither her, nor custom stale her infinite variety!" Indeed not! The professor learned that day that there was nothing withered or stale about this refreshing woman.

At the age of seventeen Adeline de Walt had fallen in love with Frank Reynolds, son of the mayor of Vinton. Their marriage was a happy one in spite of his improvident ways. He was a juggler on a vaudeville circuit and never had much money for his wife and four children. She never felt like blaming him, because he loved her and she had had little enough of love from her father.

In 1893, when she was thirty-one, she took her children

to Boston and enrolled for a course in dramatics at the New England Conservatory of Music, College of Oratory. Sir Henry Irving, leading Shakespearean actor of his day, offered her a place in his company; but when she learned that she would be expected to leave her children behind in the care of a nurse she promptly decided to put off the fulfillment of her dream once more. Leave her children's spiritual guidance to a procession of housekeepers and nursemaids? Never in the wide world! Her daughter, Mary Adams, writes to me that when a fine old gentleman criticized her mother for the way she was bringing up her children and said, "You treat them like royalty!" she warmly retorted: "They *are* royalty—they are the sons and daughters of God!" She believed that a mother's first responsibility was to her own offspring, and that careers should wait until that sacred duty had been performed. Her other daughter, Lelah M. Reynolds, writes: "Every evening Mother read to us children gathered about her knee. This was when I learned to love poetry—she read Whittier's 'Snow-Bound,' Scott's 'Lady of the Lake,' Lamb's 'Tales from Shakespeare,' and Kipling's Jungle Books, among many others. She would then send us to bed, kissing us on the forehead and saying, 'That is for wisdom.'" A nursemaid would hardly have left any such heritage as that!

She did not mope or moan over this unhappy choice. "I realized even then," she says, "that *one of the secrets of being happy is to enjoy whatever you are doing*, even if it isn't your cherished dream. What I had to do at the moment was to be the best mother I knew how to be. Hating your lot in life will only keep you from realizing your dream later on."

In 1905, Frank Reynolds died and left the forty-three-year-old widow to face the world alone with her four children. That first year was a hard one. Employers said she was too old for a job! Money ran so low that she even sold the pillows off the beds to provide her children at least with prunes and beans. She finally decided that if no employer would hire her, she would make a job for herself. So she took some training in secretarial work, moved to San Francisco, and set up a secretarial school.

Things were just beginning to look a bit brighter when the great earthquake of 1906 hit San Francisco and wiped out a large section of that city. Ida Ansell was in partnership with Mrs. Reynolds at the time of the fire, and this quiet little lady now lives in Hollywood. So, at my suggestion, we crossed the city for an interview. "Here we were," said Miss Ansell, "Adeline and her four children and I fleeing wildly through the rocking, burning city with other tens of thousands, Adeline with a pillowcase full of needed articles tied to the end of a pole, little Mary clutching her tiny red rocker and Lelah with a copy of Dickens' *Bleak House* under her arm."

On the edge of the doomed city they stopped to make a shelter for the night. "Although I was frightened and timid," Miss Ansell continued, "Adeline was resourceful and quiet. She leaned some boards up against a fence, gathered leaves for a bed, and in we crawled." Mrs. Reynolds's reaction when the six homeless refugees were settled for the night? "Isn't this cozy!" she said. The next day she trudged clear across the burning city to send telegrams to her relatives assuring them that the family was safe and sound with nothing to worry about!

Little Franklin was the only one in the family with any money. He had brought along the five dollars he had saved selling papers. His mother borrowed that and stretched it as far as it would go to feed her hungry brood. Soon afterward she was back in business again "on a shoestring," training secretaries for businessmen. "My girls were in great demand," says Grandma Reynolds, "because I *trained them not to be afraid*. A fearful heart always bungles. Businessmen were soon paying extra to get my girls, because I taught them so much more than typing and shorthand."

Eight years later, young Franklin suddenly died. He had been a sensitive little fellow with an understanding heart, and Mrs. Reynolds nursed her grief with such persistence that she was ill for a long time. She had been able to take all the other slings of outrageous fortune in stride, but here was something that was rapidly turning her into a wrinkled old woman. Just here, forty years ago, if I interpret her life correctly, was the turning point in her remarkable life—the place where a decision in the realm of spirit finally determined whether she would sink or swim, survive or perish.

"One sleepless night," she relates, "I thought of my mother. She had always made me feel the nearness of God, even in simple things like sun, rain, and daily bread. God to her was a loving Father, and we were his perfect little children. It came to me then that I was not his perfect child, nor was I trusting him with my grief-filled heart. So, I decided then and there that I would put my trust in him as fully as I had faith in the sun for warmth and in bread to nourish my body.

"The transformation was not instantaneous. I failed often, but I was steadily traveling in the right direction. I grew younger in heart, and I looked younger, too. I no longer saw myself as a woman bereft and alone, but as God's child receiving the gift of time to dig my talent out of the ground." That parable of the talents means a lot to this gallant lady.

"We all have been given certain talents," she said to me on a streetcar, "but if we let grief, disappointment, or frustration cause us to bury them in the ground, we lose them. Then your dreams can't ever come true."

In 1926, at the age of sixty-four, Mrs. Reynolds decided that the time had come to make a lifelong dream come true. For half a century she had longed for a college education. Now, with her children grown up, educated, and out on their own, why not matriculate in the University of California? This she did, working her way through and graduating with honors at the age of seventy.

Now for the fulfillment of still another dream, one she had had ever since the farm days way back in Vinton: Why not become an actress? It took ten long years of grueling work to bring that one off—years that would have broken her stout heart had she not once for all, on a sleepless night, put herself unreservedly into the hands of a God who could not fail. She dieted (she still does, because her lunch ticket came to just thirty-six cents when I took her to Clifton's restaurant!) she practiced deep-breathing exercises, took fencing lessons, went resolutely through her setting-up exercises night and morning, joined a gymnasium so that she could swim, learned tap dancing and horseback riding. "You walk too straight, too erect," one of her directors recently told her. "After all, you're supposed to be playing the part of an Indian woman who is eighty years old in this picture." How like her was the apology of this ninety-year-old lady: "I keep forgetting; it is so difficult for me to act like an *old* woman."

It was not until she was eighty that Adeline de Walt Reynolds broke through the last remaining barriers to begin her life work! She told me that she hired an agent to represent her and get her into pictures. The agent asked her if she would be willing to pay for a chance to play at the "Assistance League Theater," where talent scouts were always on the prowl looking for new talent. She paid her money and took a part in "Landslide." MGM asked her to come to their studios for a screen test which resulted in her first motion picture role as Grandma Smith in *Come Live with Me*, starring Jimmy Stewart and Hedy Lamarr. This was it! She was in! It was, at long last, her big chance to prove herself in what she calls "my beloved work"; and that was all she had ever asked of God or man.

At the end of the first grueling day beneath the glaring lights, Jimmy Stewart asked, "Aren't you tired, Grandma?" Her eyes blazed: "Young man, if you had waited eighty years to do something, you wouldn't be tired!" When she came out of an Arizona desert recently after helping to make *Pony Soldier*, a New York paper reported that the whole cast came home with sprains, bruises, and colds and pretty well all-in except Grandma Reynolds. She came out "smiling and fresh as a daisy" after enjoying every minute of it.

Director Joseph Newman thinks her "the most refreshing actress" he has worked with in Hollywood. "Her enthusiasm is contagious," he says. "She saturates the entire troupe with spirit . . . she is the most invigorating personality you can imagine."

Well, that's the story in brief of one of the most incredible personalities of our age. What is her secret alchemy? First of all, it is her absolute and unquestioning faith in the goodness and eternal presence of God. She is a part of it, as a bay is a part of the ocean. She has shed all worry as an autumn tree sheds its leaves. Her oft repeated "God bless you" comes from her heart. In the next place, she always stands foursquare facing the future with hope and faith. She dismissed her agent recently, she told me, because he wouldn't consent to her appearing on television. "Why, that is the new medium of the future," she exclaimed, "and I intend to grow up with it. I've been on fifteen times so far, and I'm just getting started."

She loves everybody. "Selfishness makes a heart dry up inside, and a dry heart keeps no vision. As the years roll by, I would like to be not only a grandmother on the screen, but a grandmother to anybody in the world that needs me." She is, too. As I helped her off a streetcar one day, she stepped lightly down and stopped. "Let's wait for a moment so you can help that young colored mother off. She's carrying a big baby and might stumble," she said. And while I gladly complied, she stood there flashing a big smile full of all the love and understanding in the world. Her postman's little dog arrives at her door each morning five minutes ahead of his master, "because he knows I'll have a nice bowl of milk ready for him." Her love encompasses all of God's creatures.

She sees everything! On a bus one day she said to me, "Did you see that pretty girl that just got on?" I hadn't. Ten minutes later: "Did you see those eight girls file past? Four were pretty, two were dumb and two were bored with living." I hadn't noticed. Five minutes later, however, I leaned over and said, "Wow, Grandma! Look at that gorgeous redhead getting on!" She fairly beamed. "That's better, Lewis. Now you are beginning to wake up!" No wonder her doctor said to me later that morning: "She has the blood pressure of an eighteen-year-old girl! I simply can't believe the dial on the instrument."

Here are a few of Grandma Reynolds's sayings:

"From the time I was fifty, I've been growing younger."

"It is never too late to make your dreams come true."

"Know what you want to do, then stick to it until it's done."

"Forget dates and years! I never can remember them, and I don't want to." (I was with her the week she was ninety, and she wouldn't even talk about it.)

"Think how many good things you miss by doubting beforehand."

"Thinking is what we need in this world. Children should be taught to THINK." (She asked me to put that in capitals!)

"The secret of success is faith, prayer, and gratitude, backed up with hard work and eagerness for tomorrow."

"Work is one of the great secrets of being happy."

"I only need to take one step at a time." (This was said when someone questioned whether a certain distance was not too long a walk for her.)

In studying these remarkable maxims, I have been asking myself if there is an underlying philosophy of life that ties them all together. I think there is. Jesus said that if we were ever to enter the kingdom of heaven, we should have to become as little children. A child has no past and no future. His is the vital, living present. When a child plays, he plays; when he eats, he eats; when he sleeps, he sleeps. He does everything with all his might. He is gloriously *alive.*

So it is with Grandma Reynolds. When she said to me that she had never had any problems, only challenges, she meant it. With faith and hope and love, with complete reliance on an ever present Heavenly Father, she has lived each moment of her life with the zest of a little child, and as a result has homed her spirit in the midst of the radiance and glory of the kingdom of heaven. Her favorite verse of Scripture is revealing: "They that wait upon the Lord shall renew their strength; they shall mount up with wings as eagles; they shall run, and not be weary; they shall walk, and not faint."

I am sure that she has but a faint conception of her enormous influence for good in millions of lives, in spite of the large amount of mail that gladdens her heart. One woman in New York City wrote to her that, in a moment of utter despair, she had gone into her kitchen with her children, closed doors and windows, and turned on all the gas jets. Her husband was unfaithful and a drunkard, and she was without support of any kind. As she stood waiting for the end, she glanced down and saw a copy of the *Reader's Digest*. The caption that caught her eye was, "The Heart That Did Not Break." She snatched it up and read Grandma's story even as her head began to swim. Just in time she reached out and turned off the gas, telling herself: "If Grandma can do it, so can I." And she has rebuilt her life on foundations of faith and love.

Dr. Robert E. Speer, in a memorial to Louise Stockton Andrews in *One Girl's Influence*, gives her credit for the following deeply impressive lines which could have been written with Grandma Reynolds in mind:

Once only in the vast circle of time,
  Shall I move mid these scenes so cherished,
But deeds that I do, poor or sublime,
  Shall stand till the world hath perished.

Shall stand! And faces I never shall see,
  And lives that I cannot guess,
Shall be faithful or false because of me,
  Shall curse the world—or bless.

Think! I! So weak and frail and small
  This deathless power am given,
That by word or deed a host may fall,
  Or a legion be raised to heaven.

Silent Communion for Living a Long, Fruitful, Happy Life

I, too, am God's own child. I am surrounded, night and day, by his protecting, sustaining love and vitality. There is no longer any room for worry or fear. I believe, with all my soul, that if I wait upon the Lord I shall renew my strength; that I shall indeed mount up with wings as eagles; that I shall run, and not be weary; that I shall walk, and not faint.